Traditional Photographic Effects

with

Adobe®

Photoshop®

Michelle Perkins *&* **Paul Grant**

AMHERST MEDIA, INC. ■ BUFFALO, NY

D0825894

Acknowledgments . . .

The authors would like to thank Jeff Smith and Rick Ferro for generously contributing their images to this volume. In addition to being excellent photographers, Jeff and Rick are also respected authors. Their instructional books on wedding and portrait photography are highly recommended. More information on these appears in the last pages of this book.

We would also like to thank our own models for fearlessly allowing us to manipulate their images. They are: Kathryn K. and Liam K. Neaverth, Madeleine Lynch-Johnt, Christopher Puchalski, Declan O'Leary and Matthew Kreib.

Finally, thank you to our families and friends, whose constant support makes us feel very lucky, indeed.

Copyright ©2002 by Michelle Perkins and Paul Grant.
Contributing Photographers: Jeff Smith (pgs. 36–41, 63–67, 101–4), Rick Ferro (pgs. 77–80, 86–93)
All other photographs by the authors.
All rights reserved.

Published by:
Amherst Media, Inc.
P.O. Box 586
Buffalo, N.Y. 14226
Fax: 716-874-4508
www.AmherstMedia.com

Publisher: Craig Alesse
Assistant Editor: Barbara A. Lynch-Johnt

ISBN: 1-58428-056-5
Library of Congress Card Catalog Number: 00 135900

Printed in the Korea.
10 9 8 7 6 5 4 3 2 1

No part of this publication may be reproduced, stored, or transmitted in any form or by any means, electronic, mechanical, photocopied, recorded or otherwise, without prior written consent from the publisher.

Notice of Disclaimer: The information contained in this book is based on the author's experience and opinions. The author and publisher will not be held liable for the use or misuse of the information in this book.

Table of Contents

Section 3
Output Techniques

Introduction

. . . you'll never make an error that means starting over . . .

When you think of digital image manipulation, you may envision wild-looking composites (grandma with a monkey on the moon) and highly stylized photographs (that snapshot of the Grand Canyon turned into a mosaic). While these effects are a lot of fun to play with, Photoshop is also an ideal tool for photographers looking to create more traditional images.

Instead of spending hours in the darkroom laboriously dodging and burning, you can now use the superior control offered by digital dodging and burning (and since every operation can be reversed, you'll never make an error that means starting over). Want an easy way to try out handcoloring on an image? Photoshop is the answer. You can try color after color, in every intensity you can imagine, and never need to start over with a new print (plus, there's never any messy cleanup).

In this book you will learn how these traditional photographic looks can be achieved using digital techniques, which are more efficient, effective, and (best of all) foolproof. The end result will be an improvement in the quality of your images, reduced time spent retouching, and the ability to achieve a wide array of effects normally accomplished in the camera, with filters, in the darkroom, etc. With Photoshop, you'll have the tools to apply techniques and create images that would be prohibitively time-consuming (or flat-out impossible) using traditional methods.

▶ What You Need to Know

This book is designed for readers who already have a basic knowledge of Photoshop. To use these techniques, you should know how to open and save documents, create and use layers, make selections, use the paint and airbrush tools, etc. If you are new to Photoshop, completing the very effective tour and training manual on the CD that is packaged with Photoshop will be immensely helpful.

There are also a number of excellent Photoshop manuals on the market. Look for one with sample exercises that will allow you to test and solidify your new skills as you acquire them. A list of suggested titles is provided at the end of this book.

▶ Photoshop: Which Version?

There are numerous versions of Photoshop in use today—from the limited version (Photoshop LE) commonly packaged with scanners and printers, to the full professional versions (numbered Photoshop 4.0, 5.1, etc.). This book can be used successfully with Photoshop 4.0 or later (especially if you know the software reasonably well), and is specifically tailored for Photoshop 6.0. If you are using an earlier version of the program (or Photoshop LE), and are serious about making digital imaging a component of your business or art, it's time to consider upgrading. The additions to recent versions make the software well worth the investment. For a detailed description of the full features, visit the Adobe website at <www.adobe.com> (also the place to check for free downloads to make your software run its best).

▶ Organization

This book is organized into three sections. The first covers the basic methods used to get images into your computer. The second section teaches you how to use Photoshop to achieve effects normally created with traditional photographic equipment. The techniques are not presented in any special order, and do not need to be used in sequence. Each section contains complete instructions for accomplishing the effect. In the final section, you'll learn options for outputting your images.

There are numerous versions of Photoshop in use today . . .

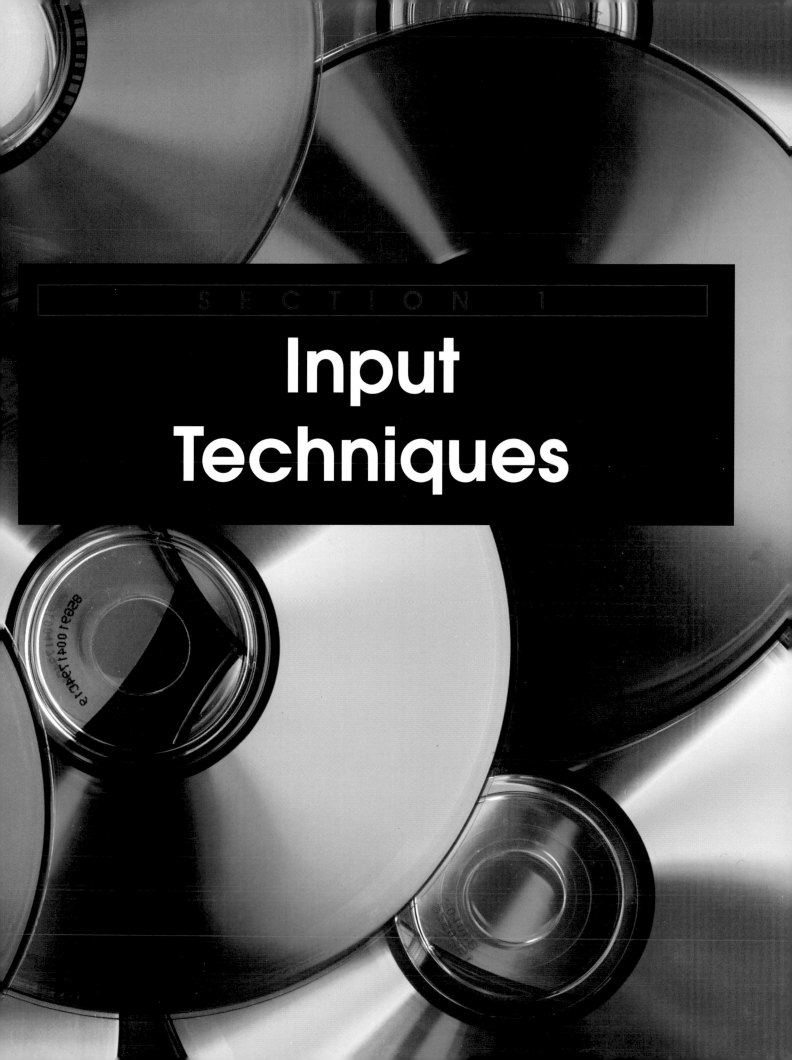

Input Techniques

Input Techniques

Inputting images into your computer is the first step in digital imaging and the foundation upon which the image stands. There are four common methods for getting an image onto your computer for manipulation and output. These are:

1. Scan it yourself with a home/office/professional scanner.
2. Have the image scanned by a service provider with equipment (such as a drum scanner) that is generally out of the price range of most individuals.
3. Have your images scanned to a Kodak PhotoCD, Kodak Photo Disc, or placed for download on the web.
4. Shoot your photograph with a digital camera.

▶ Scan It Yourself

Starting with a good scan is a key component to successful digital imaging. Plan to spend the time you need to learn the software packaged with your scanner, and master the general guidelines for good scanning.

Resolution

If your images will be viewed on the screen only (say, on a website), just about any consumer-grade scanner will be able to deliver the needed quality. If your images will be used in professional printed materials (catalogs, books, magazines, etc.), you'll need a better quality scanner. To establish the minimum performance requirements you'll need, consult with your printer about his/her needs. If you'll be outputting to a photo-quality inkjet printer, consult its manual.

Scanning Technique

In scanning, an ounce of prevention during the input process will be much better than a pound of cure. Correcting a poorly input image is rarely worth the time it takes (and almost never 100% successful). It makes sense to select the best input method in the

Starting with a good scan is a key component to successful digital imaging.

Quick Tip

A pixel is a pixel is a pixel, right? Well, not really. Not all pixels are created equal—and their differences are linked to the issue of bit depth when selecting a scanner (or a digital camera). First, a "bit" is computer-speak for the smallest morsel of information your computer can process. For devices that run on a binary system, a bit is represented by either a 0 or a 1. This means that one bit represents the choice between two states—0 or 1. Thus, a bit can be represented as a power of two—one bit equals 2^1 (two choices), two bits equals 2^2 (four choices), eight bits equals 2^8 (256 choices), and so on. Pixels (a term coined from the words "**pic**ture" and "**el**ement") have different abilities to display color, and this difference is expressed in terms of their bit depth (the number of bits per pixel). This number is, in turn, related to the total number of colors that can be displayed. For example, four bits per pixel (2^4) yields 16 colors (16 choices), while 16 bits per pixel (2^{16}) yields 65,536 colors (65,536 choices). By the time we get up to 36 bits (2^{36}), we are talking about pixels that are able to display well over a million colors—generally a requirement for creating digital color photographs.

first place, and make every effort to avoid preventable flaws in the input image.

One very common, very preventable flaw is dust on the surface of the image. Invest in some dust-free cloths and wipe down the scanner glass and the surface of the image before every scan. It may seem like a lot of trouble to go to—but it's nothing compared to the time it takes to remove hundreds of tiny specks of dust from your digital image. Some software products are available to help correct for dust in scans; Photoshop even has a filter (dust and scratches) to help eliminate problems. These do indeed work, but there can be a trade-off in image quality, so use them cautiously.

Another pesky problem can be solved with a little extra attention to detail. Sooner or later you'll scan an image, spend hours perfecting it and then realize you had the scanner set at too low a resolution. No matter how many times you've used the software, it pays to take a second before each scan and review the settings to make sure you'll get what you want.

Finally, while the world of digital imaging offers a lot of opportunity to correct flaws in images, you'll still be happiest when you start with the best possible original. Sometimes there isn't a good original to scan (often, that's why we're scanning it to begin with). But, if you have a choice between two versions of the same image, scan the best one. Keep in mind that it is easier to darken an image than to lighten it, so if you have to choose between a slightly underexposed (dark) original and a slightly overexposed (light) original, go with the overexposure.

And finally, don't forget that you can always re-scan. When the first scan comes up on your screen, take a good look at it. Check out the resolution (by going to Image>Image Size), examine the highlight and shadow areas to see if the detail you want has been captured. If you're not convinced it's the best scan you can get with your equipment, try again.

Scanning is an art, and the more you use your equipment, the better you'll get at anticipating the results.

▶ Scans by Service Providers

Scanning services are offered by various types of companies, from printers, to photo-finishers, to specialized service providers. You can purchase scanning services on the Internet, or look in your local phone book for companies in your area.

If professional scanning has one big advantage it's the quality of the results. Using equipment (like drum scanners) that is far out of the price range of individual users, these companies can provide top quality scans that are clean, crisp, and brilliant. If money were no object, this is how we'd all do our scans. Unfortunately, if professional scanning has one big drawback it's the cost. Even rather small drum scans (small image files) can cost you upward of $40 each. If you need the quality (or have no financial restrictions whatsoever) you may find it well worth the price. If you have a large job to do and require this quality scan, it pays to shop around, as prices can vary widely.

▶ ProPhotoCDs, PhotoCDs, PhotoDiscs, etc.

For those of us who haven't won the lottery and/or don't need ultrahigh-quality scans (we want to use our images in books, magazines, the Internet, or photo-quality prints), there's a happy middle ground. Thousands of independent service providers offer the Kodak PhotoCD/PhotoDisc products, which provide solid, high quality scans at a pretty reasonable price.

For small jobs, PhotoCDs still aren't as economical as scans you make yourself, but for large ones (say with twenty or more images) they can become very appealing. Most PhotoCD providers also offer a quick turnaround time (often as little as 24 hours), which can be useful if you need images in a hurry or just don't have hours to sit in front of your scanner. Finally, if you rarely need to scan transparent materials, or prefer not to invest in a scanner that will handle them, you can send them out to be scanned to PhotoCD.

When shopping for a company to scan your images to PhotoCD, you'll need to have your end product in mind and know the size of the image (the dimensions in pixels) you need. For jobs where the images will be used at small sizes and/or low resolutions, the PhotoDisc or PhotoCD may suffice. These products offer smaller image sizes and lower costs per scan. For bigger jobs (where you need large, higher resolution images), the ProPhotoCD offers this, but at a higher cost per scan.

For details on precise costs, resolutions, etc., you can visit the Kodak website, or talk with the service providers you consider using. Again, pricing may vary widely, so shop around before settling on one company.

▶ Digital Cameras

While digital cameras haven't made film obsolete (yet), they have become an extremely viable tool for photographers in many fields —from photojournalism to portraiture. Even in specialties like wedding photography, where medium format is the standard, photographers are finding that the new digital cameras can achieve results that meet professional standards. For that reason, digital cameras aren't just a neat toy anymore and warrant consideration from anybody interested in digital imaging.

Image size (expressed in the number of pixels in height and width) is the holy grail of digital cameras. If you decide to buy, keep your highest-quality product in mind. Prices jump exponentially with increased image size. This isn't a time to be tempted by a bargain basement model, however, since digital images simply don't offer the same enlarging options as film. You'll also need to evaluate the camera's viewscreen, lens options, battery life, convenience and compatibility of storage options, and look for any other special features you may want.

Ultimately, even if a digital camera doesn't save you money, you may find it worthwhile simply for the convenience of the instant images it provides.

For small jobs, PhotoCDs still aren't as economical as scans you make yourself . . .

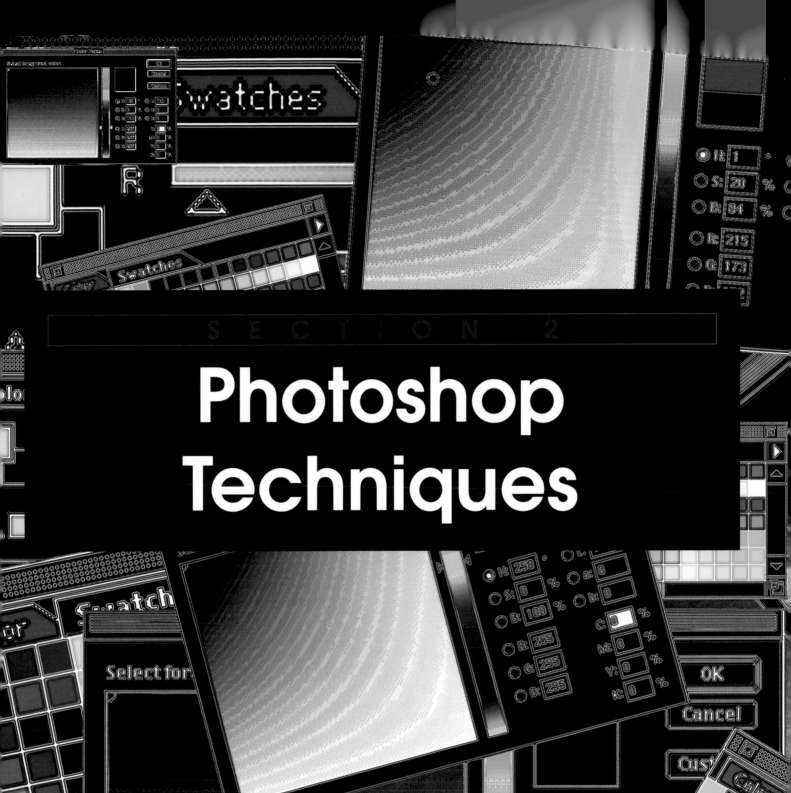

Photoshop
Techniques

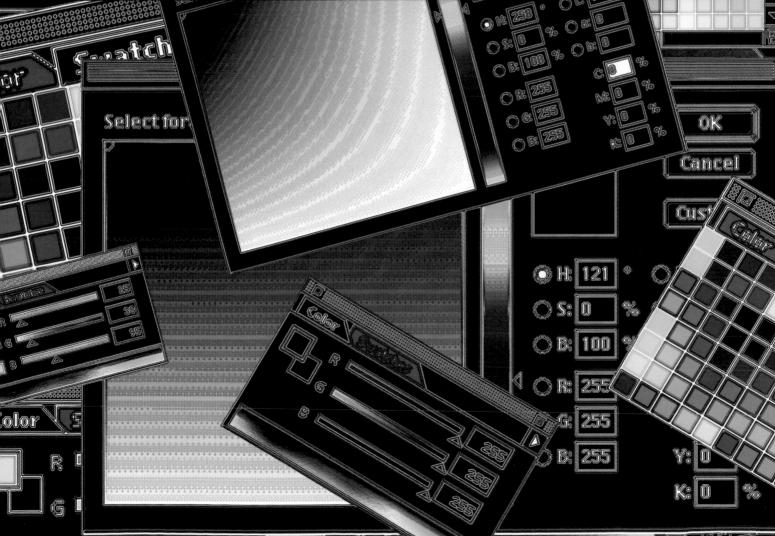

Photoshop Techniques

▶ Organization

The techniques in this section are presented in no particular order. All feature start-to-finish instructions for each effect, so there is no need to read or work sequentially. Use whatever techniques suit your taste and make your images look better.

For each image, be sure to note carefully the color mode settings given in the first step of the procedure. Not all filters work in all modes, so it is important to work in the one(s) stated. If you plan to use your final image in another mode, make the image alterations as stated, then convert the image to the necessary mode.

▶ Notation

Shortcut keystrokes are available for many common Photoshop operations (such as cutting and pasting). If you know them, use them. If you want to learn them, refer to any Photoshop manual. Because the keystroke commands differ somewhat from the Macintosh to PC versions of the program, they have been omitted here. Instead, the full menu/palette command is provided.

▶ Safety

It is *always* a good idea to keep a copy of your original, unaltered image. After all, a week down the road you may decide you don't like the changes you made and want to start over (that you can do so easily is part of the beauty of digital imaging). Also, if you've worked on many layers to create a final image, do yourself a favor and save an *unflattened* copy of your work. This gives you the option to fine-tune your changes later on without having to start from scratch.

Quick Tip

If you ever reach a point where you can't tell if you're helping or hurting the image, try this. Open up your original, unaltered image and place it side-by-side with your retouched one on the screen. Then walk away for a few minutes. Get a cup of coffee, make a phone call, and give your eyes and brain a rest. When you return to your image with a fresh set of eyes, you'll probably be able to tell right away what needs to be done. If you're still not sure, put it away for a few days and reconsider to the problem at that point.

TECHNIQUE 1
SEPIA (AND OTHER) TONING

▶ **Overview**

Toning an image adds overall color. This effect is normally used with black & white images, but your imagination is the only limit. The most commonly added tone is probably sepia (a brownish tone), but don't stop there—you can add any tone you like with Photoshop. Try out as many colors as you like before deciding, and adjust the intensity of the effect precisely to your liking without having to toss out a single print. Two "traditional" looks are demonstrated on the following pages.

▶ **Technique**

1. Begin with a digital image in the RGB mode (Image 1).

Image 1

Quick Tip

Scanners often don't produce a truly neutral scan of a grayscale image. To create one, switch your image to the Grayscale mode (Image>Mode> Grayscale). This will remove all color information. Then use the Image>Mode>RGB command to return the image to the color mode you'll need to work in to make the adjustments described in this technique.

2. Open the hue/saturation control panel (Image>Adjust> Hue/Saturation). Click the box to make your changes in the colorize mode (Image 2). Having the preview box activated will also be very helpful.

Image 2

Having the preview box activated will also be very helpful.

3. Adjust the sliders to create whatever color (hue) and intensity of color (saturation) you like. Adjusting the lightness slider will adjust the overall lightness of the image, which you can also do as you see fit. For the example shown in Image 3, the hue was set to **23**, and the saturation to 18. This creates a sepia effect.

Image 3

Adding a blue cast creates another nice look for black & white photographs. To do this, follow steps 1–3 as above (remembering to click on the colorize box), but set the sliders to hue=233, saturation=10, and lightness=0 (Image 4).

Image 4

Of course, these numbers may be changed to create whatever intensity or color effect you'd like, and to match the color profile of your output device (be it monitor, inkjet printer or negative) (Image 5).

. . . create whatever intensity or color effect you'd like . . .

Image 5

► Variations
Duotone Images

Duotone printing is a process in which two inks are used (as opposed to the single ink used in much black & white printing, or the four inks used in most color printing). Typically, duotone printing involves the use of black ink plus one colored ink. When applied to photos, creating a duotone results in a toned look.

1. Begin with a digital image in the grayscale mode (Image 6).

2. Change the image mode of the photograph to duotone (Image>Mode>Duotone).

3. When you switch to duotone, a duotone options dialogue box will appear. From the box you can select the colors of ink you want to use, and how you want to apply them (Image 7).

4. To select a tone (an ink) for your image, just click on the bottom color swatch box (indicated in Image 7 by the red arrow). This will bring up custom color dialogue box (Image 8).

Image 6

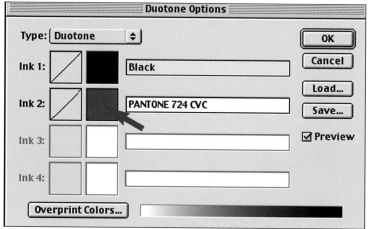

Image 7

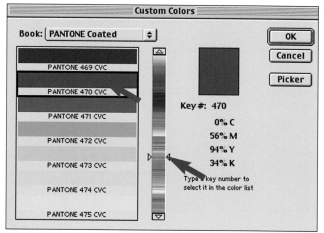

Image 8

5. Use the slider (indicated by the red arrow) to pick the approximate color you want. You can then scroll up and down through the individual colors (blue arrow). Click on the color you want. The preview is immediate, so you can try out a lot of options before making a final decision (Images 9–11). (The pull-down menu at the top of the box is labeled "Book" and allows you to select from different systems of color inks used by professional printers. Unless you are going to be printing this image with a professional printer, don't worry about this setting. If you *are*, consult with your printer on how he recommends you set up the image.) Once you have selected the color you like, hit OK.

6. If you refer to Image 7, you'll see a small curves box to the left of the color swatch next to each ink. Clicking on this will allow you to precisely control how the duotone appears (Image 12). To lighten the effect, draw the center of the curve down. To darken it, draw the center of the curve up. To change how the second

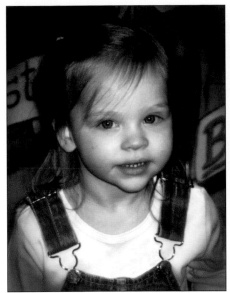

Image 9

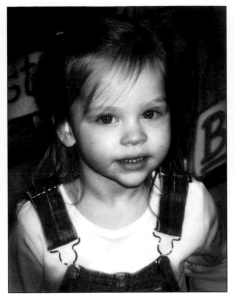

Image 10

Image 11

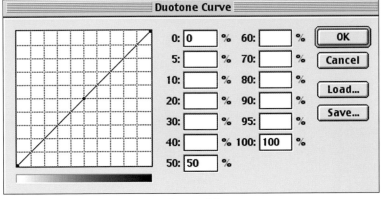

Image 12

color is applied to the highlights or the shadows, move the ends of the line.

7. When you are satisfied, hit OK. This will return you to the duotone options palette. Hit OK again, and your duotone setup is complete. If you will be printing this image yourself, you may want to experiment with printing images in the duotone mode. If you are not happy with the results, you can always switch the image to RGB (Image>Mode>RGB).

Quick Tip

To create the look of a dyed photograph, start with an image in any color mode. Go to Image>Adjust>Hue/Saturation. In the hue/saturation dialogue box, click on the colorize box to activate it. With this done, you can simply adjust the hue, saturation and lightness sliders until you have achieved the look you want.

TECHNIQUE **2**
SANDWICHED IMAGES

● ●

▶ Overview

Sandwiching images involves printing (or projecting) two images simultaneously on one piece of paper (or projection screen). The result is rather like a double exposure.

In Photoshop, you can achieve the identical effect, but with quite a bit more control (and a whole new set of creative options). Sandwiching is a good technique for adding a little

The result is rather like a double exposure.

Image 1

"something" to an image, or to contrast two images in one frame. In the example provided, the sandwiching technique was used to contrast ancient artifacts from Europe and North America.

The effect can be performed using any two (or even more) digital images, and works well in either black & white or color. For the most options, work with images in the RGB mode (even if you intend your final product to be black & white). For the best results, you may want to use one photo of a subject (a person, object, landscape), and one more abstract photo (a texture, close-up of foliage, etc.). This will minimize the possibility that the image will become too confusing for viewers to understand.

At the end of this section you'll also get some ideas for generating your own images to sandwich with your existing digital images—without digging out your camera.

A few interesting variations follow the basic technique.

▶ Technique
1. Begin with an image in the RGB mode (Image 1).
2. Copy and paste a second image into a new layer (Image 2).

The effect can be performed using any two (or even more) digital images . . .

Image 2

3. At the moment, the second image will completely obscure the first image. There are several ways to reveal the image that lies underneath.

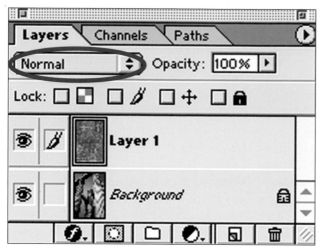

Image 2

One way is to adjust the layer mode to something other than normal (Image 3).

Image 3 (multiply)

> There are several ways to reveal the image that lies underneath.

Depending on the look you want, this simple change may produce intriguing results (Images 4–10).

Image 4 (overlay)

Image 5 (hard light)

Image 6 (color dodge)

Image 7 (color burn)

Image 8 (difference)

Image 9 (hue)

Image 10 (screen)

4. Another way is to adjust the opacity of the new layer. The control for this is in the upper part of the layers palette (Image 11). In Image 12, the new layer was set in the normal mode, and to 70% opacity. In Image 13, the opacity was changed to 50%. The opacity can be changed with layers of any mode, however.

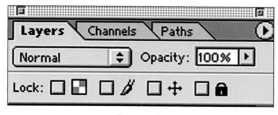

Image 11

Image 12 (70% opacity)

Image 13 (50% opacity)

5. Finally, you may wish to make additional adjustments (Image 14) using the layer style palette (Layer>Layer Style>Blending Options).

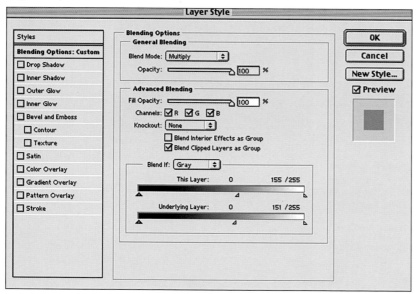

Image 14

In this case, blending changes were made to the blue channel (but you can also experiment with the other channels). Image 15 shows the results of setting the blend mode to multiply and the fill opacity to 100%. In Image 16, the blue channel was blended as shown above (this layer=155/255, underlying=151/255).

Image 15

Image 16

Quick Tip

You may not wish to create a sandwiched negative effect throughout the frame. If so, select the areas where you do not want the sandwiching to occur. Activate the new layer and clear these areas (Edit> Clear) to leave the underlying image unobscured (unchanged) as you refine your settings for the overlying layer.

▶ Variations
Making Your Own Images to Sandwich

You might not always have the right second image to add to an existing photograph. If so, consider making your own image. Since the new image will be used in a semi-transparent state, it doesn't have to be a masterpiece.

One method for creating an image to sandwich is to open a new document in Photoshop, and start drawing. Create random shapes and lines in assorted colors, then run one or more filters on the image to "abstract" it.

You can also use your scanner to create images of relatively flat things. It works just like a digital camera with its own built-in light source! Just place fabric, leaves, paperclips, etc., on the glass and scan an image of the size and resolution you need to sandwich with another photo. Be very careful never to place items on the scanner glass that could break or scratch it.

TECHNIQUE 3
SIMULATED INFRARED

▶ Overview

Black & white infrared film is sensitive to infrared radiation as well as the full spectrum of visible light. Because infrared waves are not absorbed or reflected in the same quantities as visible light, infrared images appear much different than regular black & white photographs. This effect is enhanced by the use of a dark red or opaque filter, which absorbs most of the visible spectrum of light and allows the infrared light to make most of the exposure on the film.

Foliage and skin record as white on infrared film because they reflect infrared waves efficiently, as do clouds. Blue skies record as very dark, since the light from them is mostly absorbed by the use of the red or opaque filter. Very light objects are often surrounded with a diffuse glow (halation), which is one of the hallmarks of infrared photographs. Additionally, infrared film has a very grainy look that softens detail and provides an overall texture.

If you've ever shot infrared film, you know that it must be loaded into your camera in total darkness and that rating the film speed correctly is a problem. It is usually recommended that you bracket at least +½ stop, +1 stop and -½ stop, -1 stop for each shot. Even then, the results can be unpredictable, since you simply can't *see* how much infrared radiation is present when you are shooting.

Simulating the look of infrared in Photoshop is remarkably easy.

▶ Technique

1. To begin, select a color image (you *must* start with a color image for the technique to work). A good candidate to start with is a photograph taken outdoors of green grass and trees, such as Image 1. Set the image mode to RGB (Image>Mode>RGB).

2. Duplicate the background layer (Layer>Duplicate Layer), and name this layer "channel layer." (Image 2)

Image 1

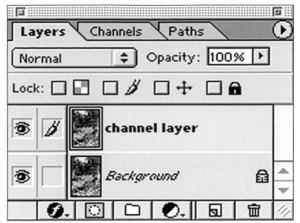

Image 2

3. With the new, duplicated layer activated, activate the channel mixer (Image>Adjust>Channel Mixer).

4. Click the "monochrome" box at the lower left of the box. This will set the output channel to black. Next, set the red slider to -70%, the green slider to +200% and the blue slider to -30% (Image 3). You should see the infrared effect begin to appear (Image 4).

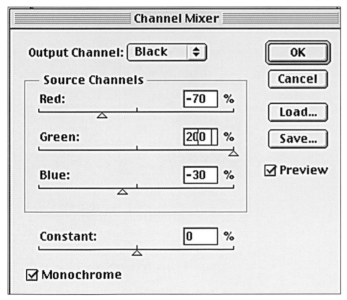

(Above) Image 3

(Right) Image 4

5. With the "channel layer" still activated, switch from the layers palette to the channels palette (View>Channels). Select the green channel (Image 5).

Image 5

6. Next we'll give the image its characteristic infrared glow. With the green channel still activated, go to Filter>Blur>Gaussian Blur and select a blur of 5.0 pixels (Image 6).

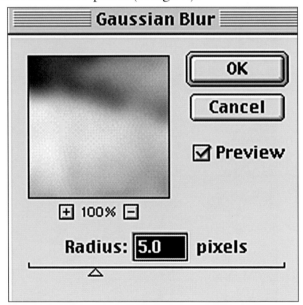

Image 6

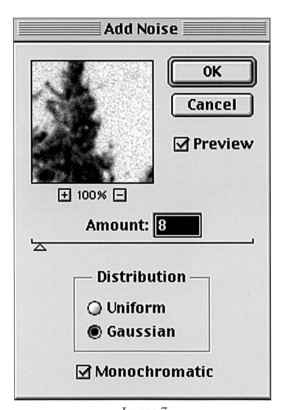

Image 7

7. This will destroy all focus in the image, so after applying the blur, go to Edit>Fade Gaussian Blur and reduce the effect to about 25–35% range, depending on your preference.

8. You can now flatten the image (Layer>Flatten Image), and convert it to grayscale (Image>Mode>Grayscale) if you wish.

9. The final touch (which may be applied to whatever degree you like, or not at all) is to add an increased appearance of grain. To do this, go to Filter>Noise>Add Noise (Image 7). Choose

Gaussian from the buttons at the bottom of the box. If working in RGB or CMYK, click the "monochrome" button at the bottom of the box.

Your final image should look something like Image 8. As you can see, this represents a significant difference from a straight grayscale conversion (Image 9).

Image 8

Image 9

▶ Final Touches

The dead giveaway that this is not actually infrared may be the fact that the sky is rendered in white instead of near-black. In this case, the white sky works better because it provides definition on the tops of the trees and helps the composition. To create a more "classic" infrared sky (Image 10, next page), follow these steps:

1. Convert the image to grayscale (Image>Mode>Grayscale).

2. Select the sky area carefully.

3. Save the selection as a new channel (Select>Save Selection).

4. In the channels palette, double click on the Alpha 1 channel. Click OK in the dialogue box (the settings won't matter).

5. Deactivate the selection in the channel by clicking on it with the marquee tool.

6. Apply a Gaussian blur to the channel (Filter>Blur>Gaussian Blur). Two to five pixels will be sufficient.

7. Return to the background image in the layers palette.

8. Load the new selection (Selection>Load Selection).

9. Since there is no detail to preserve, fill the area with whatever shade of gray you like using the fill command, airbrush or any other means you wish.

10. To add clouds, use the cloud filter (Filter>Render>Clouds).

11. Adjust the brightness and contrast of the clouds (Image> Adjust>Brightness/Contrast) until satisfied.

12. Add the same amount of grain (Filter>Noise>Add Noise) as you did to the rest of the image. (*Note:* Even if you added none, carefully add enough at this point to make the newly created sky match up with the grain in the rest of the photograph).

Quick Tip

You may want to do a little dodging and burning at the edges of the sky to make the effect look as natural as possible.

Image 10

TECHNIQUE 4
SABBATIER EFFECT (SOLARIZATION)

....

▶ **Overview**

The Sabattier effect (commonly called solarization) occurs when photographic paper is reexposed to light during the development process. As a result of this reexposure, the print acquires both positive and negative qualities, as well as what are called Mackie lines—glowing lines that appear between highlight and shadow areas.

Because the developing process leaves little reactive silver in these areas, the Sabattier effect has little impact on the print's shadow areas. The greatest changes occur in the highlight areas, where significant amounts of light-sensitive materials remain when the print is removed from the developer. These bright areas turn gray when solarized, but usually remain lighter than the shadow areas. In the areas in between, leftover chemical residues retard further development and result in lighter, glowing lines.

Normally produced in the black & white darkroom, the Sabattier effect is difficult to control with much precision. Photoshop offers a solarization filter that allows you to experiment with the effect more conveniently.

▶ **Technique**

1. Begin with an image in the grayscale mode. An image with good local and overall contrast is desirable. The effect will look most interesting if there are dark and light areas throughout the frame (Image 1).

2. Apply the solarization filter (Filter>Stylize>Solarize). Once the filter has been applied, you may want to experiment with adjusting the effect by going to Filter>Fade. You can adjust the opacity of the effect, or change the layer modes depending on the look you want to achieve.

3. In the case of this image, there were significant midtone areas left unaltered where it would be nice to see more of the effect

An image with good local and overall contrast is desirable.

Image 1

Image 2

Image 5

Image 6

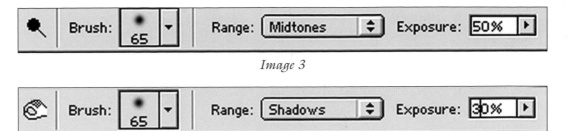

Image 3

Image 4

(Image 2). To compensate for situations like this, you can fine-tune the original to achieve the look you want.

Here, the dodge tool was set to midtones (Image 3) and a rather high exposure. This was used selectively throughout the image to brighten the midtone areas significantly (thus making them more susceptible to solarization). Then, the burn tool was set to shadow (Image 4) at a somewhat lower exposure in order to deepen the shadows in selected areas (and to deepen some of the darker midtone areas into shadows) (Image 5). This encouraged the appearance of Mackie lines, which develop between areas of strong dark and light. The resulting image (Image 6) has more local contrast (a full range of tones in any given small area).

▶ Other Options
Tonal Range
The highlights in this image now top out at a relatively dark gray. Looking at the levels (Image>Adjust>Levels), you'll see that only about half of the full tonal scale is used (Image 7).

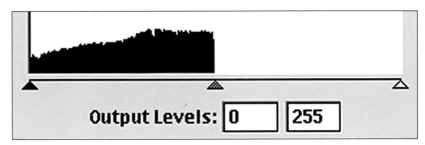

Image 7

If you'd prefer a more full range of tones, move the highlight (white) slider to the left (Image 8) until you achieve the tonal range you want (Image 9).

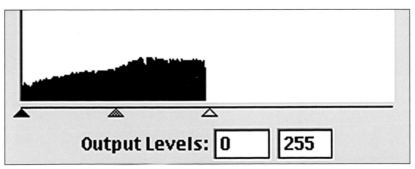

Image 8

Image 9

Color Solarization

You can also use precisely the same techniques to solarize a color photo. Just begin with an image in the RGB mode (image 10), and use the solarize filter in precisely the same manner. The results are a little strange looking, but may certainly have their uses (Image 11).

Image 10

Image 11

VIGNETTES

● ●

▶ **Overview**

Vignetting is a darkening (or, in some cases, a lightening) around the edges of an image. Sometimes this can occur accidentally (often from using a filter or lens attachment that is too small for the lens), but it is also done intentionally. Particularly in portraiture, vignetting is used to draw the viewer's eye away from the background and toward the person (presumably the reason for taking the picture in the first place).

Intentional vignetting can be done in-camera via any number of lens attachments, or in the darkroom via various masking devices. In Photoshop, vignetting is a relatively simple matter, with almost endless possibilities. The basic techniques for high key (light) and low key (dark) vignetting are detailed below. Several creative variations follow.

▶ **Techniques**

Low Key Vignetting

Low key vignetting is probably the most common type. This technique is normally applied to images where the overall subject matter is normal to dark (i.e., not a polar bear eating a marshmallow on a snowbank). It involves darkening the corners and sides of the image, making the central portion of the frame the lightest in the photo (and therefore the part the viewer's eye will be drawn to). The process is easy:

1. Begin with a color or black & white image in either the RGB or grayscale mode (Image 1). (*Note:* If you choose to work in the grayscale mode, you will only be able to create a grayscale vignette—this may be exactly what you want, but if not, convert your image to the RGB mode. You can convert is back later.)

2. The next step is more subjective, and will vary from photo to photo. Using any of the selection tools (marquee, magic wand, lasso), select the area that will *not* be vignetted (i.e., the area that

. . . draw the viewer's eye away from the background and toward the person . . .

Image 1 (original photo by Jeff Smith)

Image 2

you want to remain untouched in the final image). Normally, this will be the subject of the photograph and some of the area around it. Your selection could be a square, circle, oval, rhomboid, a heart—anything you like (Image 2).

3. With your selection activated, invert the selection (Select> Inverse). This command will select everything that wasn't in your original selection. This is the area where the vignette will be created.

If you've created any kind of complicated selection, or are just paranoid, you may want to save the selection so there's no danger of losing it accidentally. To do this, go to Select>Save Selection, and name your selection in the dialogue box. If you do accidentally deactivate your selection, you can then reload it by going to Select>Load Selection and choosing the appropriate name from the pull-down menu. Be sure to delete this selection (it will appear in the channels palette and can be dragged into the trash) when you are done. Otherwise, you will be prohibited from using the full range of file formats when you save your image.

4. With your selection still activated (but now inverted), feather the selection using the Select>Feather command (Image 3). Feathering blurs the edges of the selection so that the transition will be gradual between the vignetted and unvignetted areas of

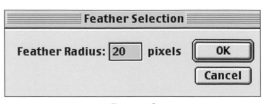

Image 3

the image. You can decide for yourself how much feathering you'll need to create the effect you want. A few examples are shown below (Images 4–9). The only difference between the images is in the amount of feathering. The selected area was filled using the Edit>Fill command and selecting black with the blending set to 50% opacity.

Image 4
(0 pixels)

Image 5
(20 pixels)

Image 6
(40 pixels)

Image 7
(60 pixels)

Image 8
(80 pixels)

Image 9
(100 pixels)

5. From this point you have a lot of options. A few variations are described below.

A. With the selection still activated, create a new layer (Layer> New>Layer). Use the Edit>Fill command to fill the selected area with the color of your choice. Reduce the layer opacity (Layer>Layer Style>Blending Options) to allow some of the underlying image to show through.

B. With the selection still activated, copy (Edit>Copy) and paste (Edit>Paste) the contents of the selected area of the image into a new layer. Using any of the tools under Image>Adjust (curves, levels, variations, brightness/contrast, etc.), you can reduce, darken, or alter the color of the selected area. You can then set the opacity of this layer as you like (Layer>Layer Style>Blending Options).

C. With the selection activated, create an adjustment layer (Layer>New Adjustment Layer) of whatever type you like (curves, layers, etc.). Darken or otherwise adjust the vignetted area with this layer, then set the opacity of the layer as you like (Layer>Layer Style>Blending Options).

D. With the selection still activated, copy (Edit>Copy) and paste (Edit>Paste) the contents of the selected area of the image into a new layer. Experiment with the layer modes (Layer>Layer Style>Blending Options) to create whatever effect you like. Image 10 shows the use of the multiply mode at 100% blending opacity—a very natural effect.

E. With the selection still activated, use the burn tool to darken the vignetted areas as you like. Try different settings to burn primarily the highlights, shadows or midtones, and to alter the exposure. With the burn tool selected, the various options are all listed in the options menu that is located at the top of the screen.

6. When you've created an effect you like, flatten the image (Layer>Flatten Image) and save it (save the unflattened version, too, if you think you might ever want to change it).

High Key Vignetting

High key vignetting is normally applied to images where the subject of the photo is the darkest thing in the frame (i.e., a polar bear eating a marshmallow on a snowbank). Even with images like these, dark vignetting may sometimes be more effective—use your judgement. High key vignetting involves lightening the corners and sides of the image, making the central portion of the frame the only dark area in the photo (and therefore the part the viewer's eye will be drawn to). The process is just as easy as creating low key vignetting:

1. Begin with a color or black & white image in either the RGB or grayscale mode (Image 11).

2. The next step is more subjective, and will vary from photo to photo. Using any of the selection tools (marquee, magic wand, lasso), select the area that will *not* be vignetted (i.e., the area that you want to leave untouched in the final image). The selection can be any shape you like.

Image 10

High key vignetting involves lightening the corners and sides of the image . . .

3. With your selection activated, invert the selection (Select> Inverse). This will select everything that wasn't in your original selection (the area where the vignette will be created).

4. With your selection still activated (but now inverted), feather the selection using the Select>Feather command. Feathering blurs the edges of the selection so that the transition will be gradual between the vignetted and un-vignetted areas of the image. You can decide for yourself how much feathering you'll need to create the effect you want. A few examples are shown below.

5. There are somewhat fewer options with lightening, presuming you are starting with an image that is already very light in the area to be vignetted. If, for some reason, you are applying a light vignette to a medium to low key image, refer to options B, C and D on page 38, but use the same tools to lighten (rather than darken) the selected area. For those starting with a light image, two variations are described below.

A. With the selection still activated, create a new layer (Layer>New>Layer). Use the Edit>Fill command to fill the selected area with white (or perhaps another very light color). You may also wish to reduce the layer opacity (Layer>Layer Style>Blending Options) very slightly to allow some of the underlying image to show through (Image 12).

Feathering blurs the edges of the selection so that the transition will be gradual.

Image 11 (Photo by Jeff Smith)

Image 12

B. With the selection still activated, use the dodge tool to lighten the vignetted areas as you like. Try different settings to dodge primarily the highlights, shadows or midtones, and to alter the exposure. With the dodge tool selected, these are all listed in the options menu that is located at the top of the screen.

▶ Variations

Soft Vignettes

Vignettes are typically somewhat out of focus. With your selection activated and your darkening/lightening complete, use the Filter>Blur>Gaussian Blur command to soften the vignette. You can also experiment with other blurs (radial blur, motion blur, etc.). Images 13 and 14 show the difference between a blurred and unblurred vignette.

*Image 13
(vignette with no blur)*

*Image 14
(vignette with 77 pixels
Gaussian blur)*

Sandwiched Vignettes

Use another image to create a vignette.

1. Select the area of the image that will *not* be vignetted.

2. Open a second image (abstract photos work best for this).

3. Select the entire second image (Select>All).

4. Copy (Edit>Copy) the image and paste (Edit>Paste) the second image into a new layer in the image where you will be creating a vignette.

5. With the selection still active, activate (by clicking on it in the Layers palette) the second image that you just pasted in.

6. Go to Edit>Clear, to make the selected area of the second layer transparent, allowing the main image to show through. (*Note:*

Quick Tip

One of the most common problems with digital images is the failure of the highlights to hold detail. As a result, when you further lighten areas that were light to begin with, you may notice "flat" areas that lack the desired detail. There are a couple of solutions. One is to completely eliminate all detail in the vignette area (create a vignette that is pure white). When this prints, only the bare paper will show in this area. Another option is to use a faintly-colored vignette so there will be some information throughout the area, regardless of loss of detail in the original image. A third option is to use a filter to add a little grain throughout the vignette (creating the impression of detail throughout). To do this, go to Filter>Artistic>Film Grain or Filter>Noise>Add Noise and experiment until you come up with a look that satisfies you. You may also wish to use the history brush to reapply detail to an area using the history palette (if you don't know how to use this very useful tool, look it up in any basic Photoshop manual—it can be a lifesaver!).

For softer edges on the vignette, use Edit>Undo to undo the last operation. Then use the feather command [Select>Feather] to blur the edge of the active selection as much or as little as you like. Then go to Edit>Clear again.) An example of this technique is shown in Image 15. In this photo, the vignette was created using a scanned image of lace.

Filtered Vignettes

Run any number of filters on your vignette to create a very different look. An example of this technique is shown in Image 16, where the wave filter was used on the vignette (Filter> Distort>Wave).

Image 15 (Photo by Jeff Smith)   *Image 16*   *Image 17*

Variation 4

Instead of a geometric vignette (like an oval), try creating a custom edge on your vignette. You can do this by using the lasso tool to make your selection, or by modifying the edges of a geometric selection by using the smudge tool, eraser, paintbrush, or another tool. An example of this technique is shown in Image 17. Here, an irregular selection was created around the subject using the lasso tool.

TECHNIQUE 6
HANDCOLORING

▶ Overview

Handcoloring black & white photos (or color ones for that matter) is usually accomplished with a variety of artistic media—pastels, watercolors, markers, oil paints, colored pencils, etc. The effect, recalling the only means of achieving a color image before the advent of color film, has an appealing timeless quality. As black & white images have experienced a resurgence in popularity in recent years, so too has handcoloring become an increasingly popular art form.

If you've ever actually colored an image by hand, you know how much time it takes—and also how easily small mistakes can have you desperately trying to remove colors with various solvents and bleaches.

With Photoshop, the process is remarkably easy—and if you goof or change your mind you can just hit Edit>Undo (or use the history palette to backtrack if you didn't notice the problem right away). For those of you who never got the hang of coloring, you can create selections or masks to help you stay inside the lines. You can also try out lots of different looks and experiment freely with colors before deciding what works best.

Image 1

▶ Techniques

Handcoloring in Photoshop can be accomplished through two basic means: the use of layers in the color mode, and the use of the the hue/saturation command. We'll begin working simply with layers, since this is the most intuitive of the two methods.

Handcoloring with Color Layers

1. Begin with a black & white image in the RGB color mode (Image>Mode>RGB). The image must be in a color mode or you will not be able to add color to it (Image 1).

2. Create a new layer (Layer>New>Layer) and set it to the color mode (Image 2).

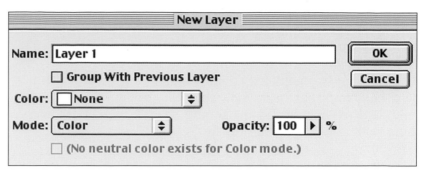

Image 2

3. Double click on the foreground color swatch in the lower section of the tools palette to activate the color picker (Image 3). Using the slider in the color picker, select the color range you want, then click on a specific spot to select the color. When you've found one you like, hit OK to select that color as the new foreground color. This is the color your painting tools will apply to the canvas. You may switch it as often as you like.

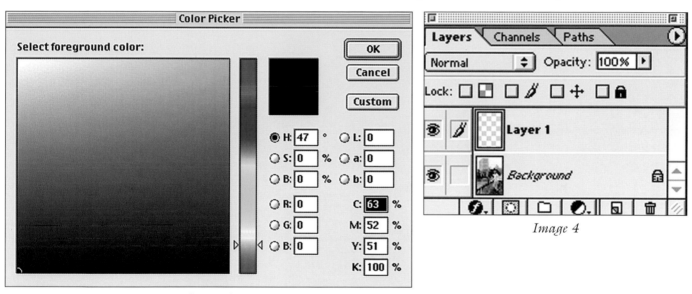

Image 3

Image 4

4. With your color selected, return to the new layer you created in your image. Click on this layer in the layers palette to activate it, and make sure that it is set to the color mode (Image 4).

5. Select the airbrush tool (or paintbrush) and whatever size brush you like, and begin painting. Because you have set the layer mode to color, the color you apply with the brush will allow the detail of the underlying photo to show through.

6. If you're a little sloppy (as in Image 5), use the eraser tool (set to 100% in the options menu) to remove the color from anywhere you didn't mean to put it. Using the magnifying glass to zoom in tight on these areas will help you work as precisely as possible.

7. If you want to add more than one color, you may wish to use more than one layer, all set to the color mode.

8. When you've completed your "handcoloring," the image may be either completely or partially colored. For this shot (Image 6) only parts of the city and the subject were colored. With everything done, you can flatten the image and save it as you like.

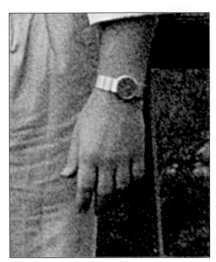

Image 5

Image 6

Handcoloring with the Hue/Saturation Mode

This method is, perhaps, a little trickier than the one previously described because it relies on your ability to make accurate selections using the marquee and magic wand tools. It works best when applying solid colors to a large area of the image (here, a building).

Quick Tips

1. For a more subtle effect, reduce the opacity of the color layer (Layer>Layer Style>Blending Options).

2. Where possible, use the selection tools (marquee, magic wand, lasso, etc.) to isolate large sections that will be colored with one solid tone (such as the tall building in the background of the photo). Then use the Edit>Fill command to fill the selected area with the foreground color of your choice.

3. If you've carefully painted a whole section on a single layer, but decide the color isn't right, don't start from scratch, use the magic wand. Click on a painted area of the layer. (If the painted areas you wish to select are not contiguous, go to Select>Similar to expand your selection to include all areas of that color.) With the selection made, you can simply select a new color and use the Edit>Fill command to fill the selection with the foreground color.

4. When handcoloring with color layers, one major obstacle is the inability to add any significant color density to very light areas of the image. Generally, color in these areas will be very pastel (or may be impossible to add if the area is pure white). Handcoloring with the hue/saturation mode will allow you to add color in these spots. Remember, you can combine both methods in the same image.

1. Begin with a black & white image in the RGB color mode (Image>Mode>RGB). The image must be in a color mode or you will not be able to add color to it (Image 1, page 42).

2. Carefully select the area of the photograph to which you will add color (Image 7).

3. Feather the selection (Select>Feather). For most purposes, feathering by two pixels will create a natural-looking transition between the selected and unselected areas. For softer transitions (say, to add a soft pink on someone's cheeks), you may need to feather the selection considerably more.

Image 7

4. With the selection made, create a new adjustment layer to adjust the hue/saturation (Layer>New Adjustment Layer> Hue/Saturation) (Image 8).

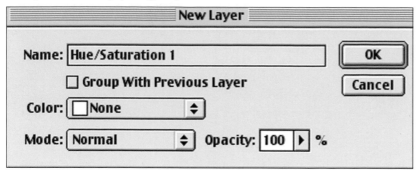

Image 8

5. Clicking OK in the new layer dialogue box will open the hue/saturation control panel (Image 9).

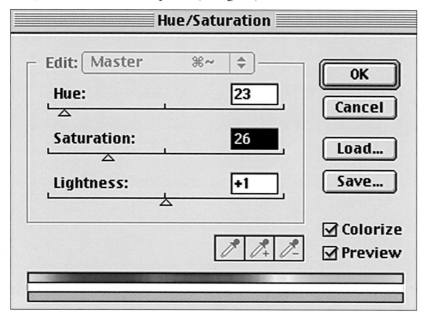

Image 9

6. Click the colorize button at the lower right of the box.

7. Slide the hue, saturation and lightness controls until you achieve the desired coloration. The hue slider moves from red, to greens, to blues as you go from left to right. The saturation slider decreases saturation when moved to the left, and increases saturation when moved to the right. To darken, slide the lightness control to the left; to lighten, slide it to the right.

8. When you have adjusted the coloration to your satisfaction, click OK.

9. Since you have applied this operation on an adjustment layer, you can adjust the layer mode and opacity from within the layers palette. Double clicking on the layer will re-open the hue/saturation panel if you decide you need to make a change.

Slide the hue, saturation and lightness controls until you achieve the desired coloration.

Quick Tips

Selecting the right colors for handcoloring can take a lot of trial and error. The following are suggestions and color "recipes" to get you started.

1. If you have a color image of the same subject you'll be handcoloring, you have a great starting point. Simply scan the image and adjust it so the color looks right. Then, use the eyedropper tool to click on an area of color you want to use in your handcolored image. This will make the chosen color your foreground color. You can then return to the image to be handcolored and begin painting with the color using any tool (pencil, airbrush, etc.). If you can leave both documents open at the same time, it's very easy to switch back and forth to pick and apply colors between the two.

2. Skin tones are notoriously difficult to match, since there is such a wide variety in the world and people who know the subject will immediately notice even small inaccuracies (after all, they see the real thing every day). The best way to match skin tones is to use the technique described above to sample the real thing from another photo, and apply it to the handcoloring job.

If this isn't possible, for caucasian skin you can start with a recipe in the neighborhood of Cyan=15%, Magenta=25%, Yellow=35% and K=0%. Simply click on the foreground color to activate the color picker, then type these numbers into the CMYK spaces on the right-hand side of the dialogue box. (This will work in any of the color modes, not just in CMYK.) You may wish to adjust this for more olive complexions, subjects with a tan, etc. Increasing the magenta slightly will give you a nice color for natural cheeks and lips. Everything should, of course, be adjusted for the individual.

3. Always remember that, unless it's been carefully color corrected to match the color profile of the output device, what you see on your monitor and your final printed result may be quite different. Until you are accustomed to predicting potential color shifts in your output, budget a little extra time for test prints—just in case.

4. There's no reason you have to select colors that are anything like the originals—green skin, orange grapes, and purple dogs may all be part of your vision for an image. Since you can experiment more easily with color using Photoshop, rather than traditional techniques, don't deny yourself the chance to play with the possibilities. It's easy to backtrack if need be.

TECHNIQUE 7
COLOR TO BLACK & WHITE (AND BASIC COLOR CORRECTION TECHNIQUES)

▶ Overview

When you print a color negative on black & white paper you'll usually notice an objectionable loss of contrast. This can be bumped up using a higher contrast paper (or contrast filters with multi-contrast paper). Much the same thing will happen if you convert a color image to grayscale in Photoshop using the Image>Mode>Grayscale command. Using this command will cause Photoshop to mix all of the original color channels into the one monochrome channel.

With a straight conversion (simply changing to the grayscale mode), you'll have the best results if the image is good to begin with—accurately color balanced, with good contrast and detail in the highlights and shadows. Images 1a and 1b show the results of converting an unaltered (no refinements to color balance or contrast) RGB image to a grayscale image. Images 2a and 2b show the overall improvement made by color correcting and contrast correcting an image before converting it to grayscale.

> . . . you'll have the best results if the image is good to begin with . . .

▶ Techniques

Professional color correction is a complex topic, and complete treatment of it falls outside the range of this book. If you plan to

---

Quick Tips

You'll be happiest when you select photos to "transform" that have a strong design and don't rely primarily on color for their impact. Obviously, this is not always possible (say, if your color photo is to be used in a newspaper and color isn't an option). In this event, using the techniques described will be especially important for creating the best possible results.

Image 1a
(straight, uncorrected scan)

Image 1b
(uncorrected image converted to grayscale)

Image 2a
(color corrected scan)

Image 2b
(corrected image converted to grayscale)

do a lot of digital imaging, or will use your digital images for CMYK printing (like books and magazines), it's a topic you'll want to devote considerable time to learning. Some helpful manuals are included in the bibliography. For those who don't want to make a career out of color correction, the following guidelines will help you to create better color originals and make better conversions to black & white.

Basic Color Corrections

For general/casual purposes (printing the photo on your inkjet printer, or using it on the web) there's room for trial and error. If that's how you'll be using your images, Photoshop offers some "automated" tools that will help you make basic corrections.

1. You may wish to try the variations tool (Image>Adjust> Variations). This allows you to select the best image from a number of slightly different previews (Image 3). You can change the degree of change visible in the previews by using the slider at the upper right corner of the dialogue box. You can also choose to look at variations in the shadows, highlights or midtones. This tool is very useful for eliminating overall color casts (such as the yellow cast in Image 1a).

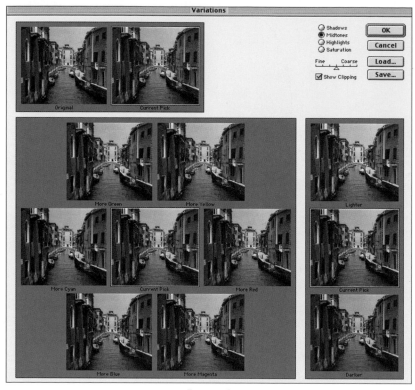

Image 3

2. You can also use the auto levels (Image>Adjust>Auto Levels) or auto contrast (Image>Adjust>Auto Contrast). These tools are fully automated (just select them and they do the rest). If you like the results—great! If not, you can simply undo them.

3. Try the brightness/contrast adjustments (Image>Adjust> Brightness/Contrast). Move the slider to the right to increase the brightness/contrast to the desired level. Watch the highlights and shadows carefully, as this tool makes it very easy to blow out light areas or block up the shadows (i.e., lose detail in these areas).

While these tools alone won't give you complete control, they will be sufficient to correct many images.

More Advanced Color Corrections

For much better control (although somewhat less intuitive techniques), you should learn to make use of the other color correction tools in Photoshop. Of these, the most commonly called upon are probably the levels and curves commands. The variations command (shown above) can also be extremely useful.

Levels

1. To open the levels dialogue box, go to Image>Adjust>Levels. This is a good place to start with most images, since looking at the histograms (the jagged black stuff) helps you get an idea of any overall problems with the image.

Image 4

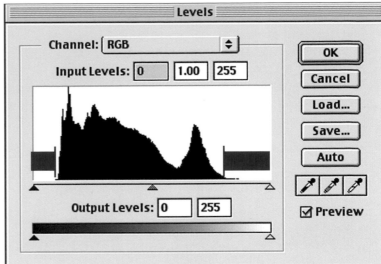

Image 5

In Images 4 and 5 you can see a photograph and its levels. The red areas added to the illustration show one of the big problems with the image—it doesn't have a full tonal range. If it did, the histogram would span the entire area between the far left black slider (black triangle) and the far right white slider (white triangle). Even if you couldn't see the image, you could look at this histogram and guess that it probably looks muddy and low in contrast (which, as you can see in Image 4, it does).

2. Correcting this problem is a simple matter of adjusting sliders. For the easiest possible correction, simply move the black and white sliders in until they line up with the closest edge of the histogram. (Images 6 and 7).

Image 6

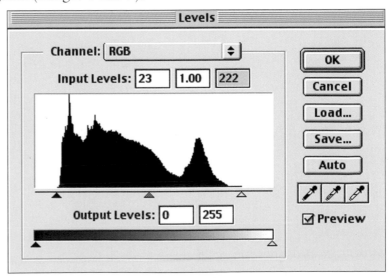

Image 7

3. However, you may have noticed that in the channels indicator in the levels dialogue box, it reads "RGB." This means that when you move the slider here, you are adjusting all of the channels identically. This is not always a problem, but to make the most accurate adjustments possible, you may wish to adjust each channel individually. This will help ensure that you are left with pure, crisp whites with very little (if any) incorrect color cast. By pulling down the RGB in the channels section of this box, you'll be able to select the individual channels (Images 8, 9, 10).

In each channel, pull the black slider to the right until it meets the very edge of the histogram. Then pull the white slider to the right until it is under the very edge of the histogram.

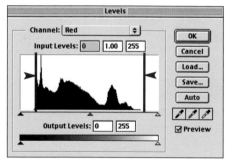
Image 8 (Red Channel)

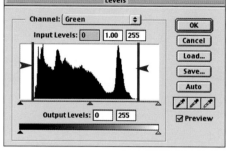
Image 9 (Green Channel)

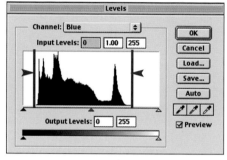
Image 10 (Blue Channel)

4. When you have corrected each channel, hit OK. Image 11 shows the finished image. It's a big improvement from what we started with, and it will look much better when converted to black & white. Adjusting the channels individually also helped to dramatically reduce the yellow cast.

Image 11

Curves

Using the curves allows you to exercise even more precise control over the color balance and contrast of your images. Like the levels, curves can be adjusted for all the channels at once or for each channel individually. It's a great place for making very fine adjustments (or for fine-tuning basic corrections made using the variations, levels, or other commands).

1. Open the curves dialogue box by going to Image>Adjust> Curves (Image 12).

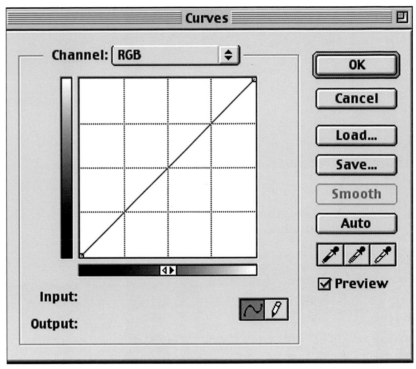

Image 12

Curves can be adjusted for all the channels at once or for each channel individually.

Unlike the levels box, the curves dialogue box will look the same for every image—a diagonal line running from dark (lower left in RGB, upper right in CMYK) to light (upper right in RGB, lower left in CMYK). The gradient tonal bars at the bottom and left of the grid show you whether that part of the diagonal line controls the shadow (dark), midtone (middle), or highlight (bright) areas of the image. The curves boxes for all of the individual channels look exactly the same, and can be accessed via the channel pull-down box at the top of the dialogue box.

2. At the lower right-hand corner of the box, you'll also see a check box marked "Preview." Leaving this box checked will allow you to instantly preview all your changes before approving them. This is extremely useful.

3. To begin experimenting with the curves, click once in the middle of the diagonal line and drag it up or down a little bit. As you'll see, the line is actually elastic and can be bent into many— you guessed it—curves. In the RGB mode, pulling up will lighten the image by increasing the lightness of the midtones (Images 13–14). Pulling the center down will darken the midtones. If you want to reverse this arrangement, click on the black/white directional arrows in the bottom gradient bar.

Image 13

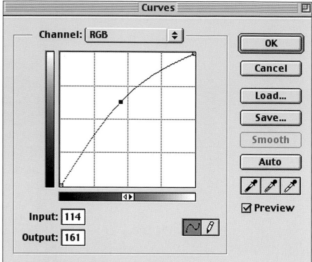
Image 14

4. By adjusting the channels individually you can also remove (or create) overall color casts (Images 15–16).

Image 15

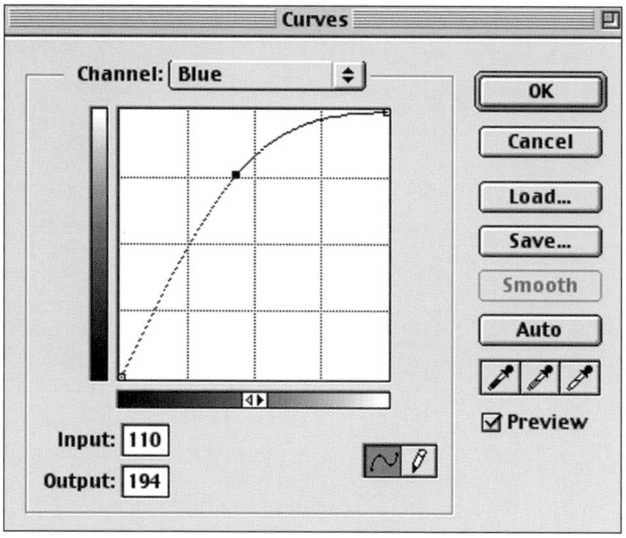

Image 16

5. You can add as many points to the curve as you want. Each time you click on the line in a new spot, a point will be created. The points can also be adjusted and released and readjusted as many times as you want. Until you hit OK and apply the changes, you can switch between channels without losing the points in any of the channels. To remove a point, simply click on it and drag it outside of the grid area.

Once you hit OK, your changes will be applied and you will not be able to go back to your adjusted curves to make further refinements. If you do re-open the curves dialogue box after hitting OK, it will look just as it did in the beginning—a straight line. Because of this, it is important to use the preview to make sure your work is the way you want it. If you're not sure (or think you'll want to use these settings again), use the save command in the curves box to store the settings. Then use the load command to restore them when needed.

6. When using the curves, unless you are going for a special look, you should keep the curves relatively small and smooth. Curves with sharp turns or an excessive number of points will usually create odd effects. Normally, a shallow C- or S-shaped curve can do the job (unless there is a serious problem with your image).

Selective Color

This is a very intuitive and useful tool for stubborn problems with a specific color or tonal range in a photo. Reds, yellows, greens. cyans, blues, magentas, whites, neutrals, and black can all be accessed from a pull-down menu at the top of the dialogue box. With the proper tonal range selected, you can simply drag the color sliders to the left or right until the colors suit you.

1. Open the selective color dialogue box by going to Image> Adjust>Selective Color.

2. Select the desired color range and adjust to your taste. You can adjust colors in every range or in one range only. You can work back and forth between the ranges without losing your settings until you apply the changes by hitting OK.

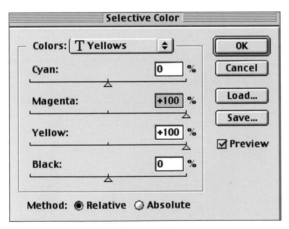
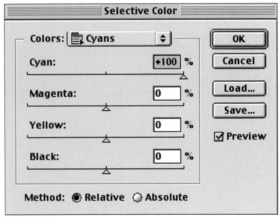

Image 17   *Image 18*

In this example, the yellows (Image 17) and cyans (Image 18) were changed dramatically (much smaller changes are more normal). You can see the result in the before (Image 19) and after (Image 20) shots, which appear on the following page.

3. When you are happy with your changes, hit OK.

Image 19

Image 20

Converting to Black & White

Once you have color corrected your image and have achieved a good tonal range and contrast, you are ready to convert the image to black & white. Just go to Image>Mode>Grayscale to make the conversion. The results should be quite good, but may still need some small adjustments.

1. Start evaluating the image by looking at the levels. As we saw when using the levels with a color image, looking at this histogram can help you to spot some overall problems (Images 21–22).

Image 21

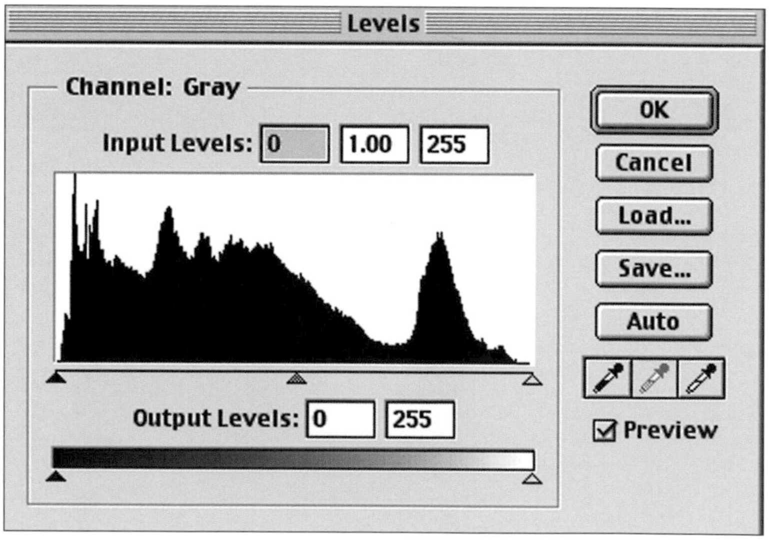

Image 22

As you can see, this looks pretty good. The histogram extends just about from edge to edge in the window, indicating that the image contains a full range of tones (from white to black).

2. However, without the colors, the image still looks a little gloomy. Brightening the midtones will frequently help the appearance of a black & white image. You can do this while you have the levels dialogue box open, by simply moving the center slider (the gray triangle) slightly to the left (Images 23–24).

Image 23

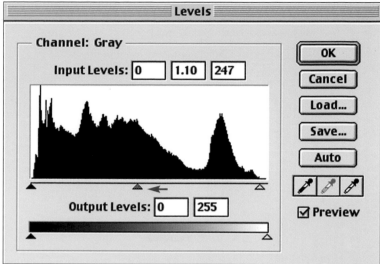

Image 24

3. Depending on your taste, you may still want to bump up the contrast a bit. You can do this in a few ways, with varying degrees of control. The easiest way is to go to Image>Adjust> Brightness/Contrast. By dragging the contrast slider to the right, you can increase the contrast. However, the contrast function applies an identical change to every pixel in the image (if you set it to +10, that change will apply universally to the shadows, high-lights and midtones). This doesn't give you much control.

4. A better way to adjust contrast is to use the curves, where you can be much more specific about where and how you build contrast. To begin, open the curves dialogue box by going to Image> Adjust>Curves (Image 25).

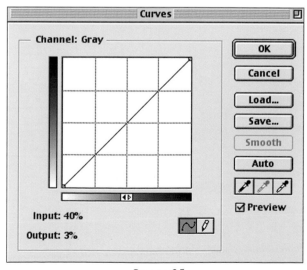

Image 25

You'll now notice that, instead of multiple channels, the image has only one channel—gray.

5. If you are happy with the midtones in the image (the middle grays don't look too dark or too light), you can nail these down by placing a point in the center of the line without moving it up or down (Image 26). (As you make your changes to the contrast, you can always adjust this, but it's a good place to start).

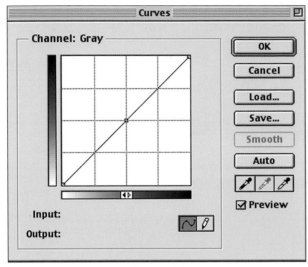

Image 26

6. To increase the contrast in the image, click on the line about halfway between the midtone and white point, and pull down slightly (Image 27). You'll see that the midpoint stays in place, while the lighter tones move toward even lighter, and the darker tones move toward even darker (use the gradient bar at the left of the grid as your guide). This yields the increase in contrast. (If you want to reduce contrast for some reason, you can do just the opposite, pulling the darker tones toward lighter and the lighter tones toward darker.)

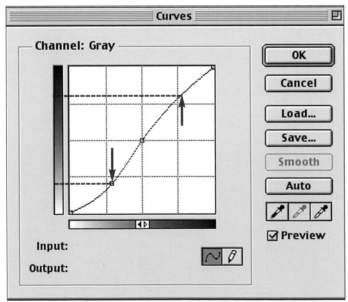

Image 27

Image 28
(before application of curves)

Image 29
(after application of curves)

In Images 28 and 29, you can see the results of applying the curve shown in Image 27. The contrast is much better. When applying curves to improve contrast, try to keep the curve itself as smooth as possible to achieve the most natural results. You can add as many points as you like, but usually two or three will be all that are needed. Also, keep an eye on the brightest highlights and darkest shadows to ensure that detail is not lost in these areas.

▶ Variations

Red/Orange/Yellow Filter (Channel Mixer Method)
What you really want from your color to black & white conversions is a crisp, classic image with nice contrast—much like the scene would have looked had you actually shot it on panchromatic black & white film with a red, orange, or yellow filter. These filters, used to compensate for panchromatic film's strong sensitivity to blue light, help to produce better overall contrast and record the scene more as the eye sees it. Starting with a correctly balanced color image will help a lot, but the conversion to Grayscale can also be further enhanced in just a few seconds.

1. This technique will be most dramatic with images that have a strong blue area (such as a blue sky). This is because this is specifically where the "filtration" that will be applied makes the most difference. The technique will be more subtle when applied to other images.

First, let's look at the color corrected starting image (Image 30) and the same image converted directly to the grayscale mode, using Image>Mode>Grayscale (Image 31). No changes or refinements have been made to the resulting black & white image. As you can see, the sky is particularly lacking in contrast.

Image 30
(color corrected image)

Image 31
(image directly converted to grayscale)

3. Instead of converting to grayscale directly, better results will be achieved by using the channel mixer to convert the image. To do this, open the channel mixer by going to Image>Adjust> Channel Mixer (Image 32). In the dialogue box, click the monochrome box at the lower left corner. This will change the output channel to gray.

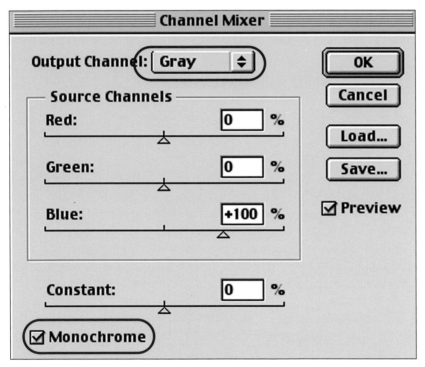

Image 32

4. Adjusting the balance of the color channels for the new monochrome image is as easy as moving the sliders. Since our goal is to make the blue tones darker (the effect of a red, orange, or yellow filter), you can start by moving the blue slider down to 0%. Then, raise the red and green sliders until their combined percentages equal 100%. You may need to adjust the blue down even further to get the look you want. However, to maintain the overall lightness/darkness of the image, make sure that all three source channels add up to 100%. In Image 33, you can see they are: Red=70%, Green=60% and Blue=-30% (70+60-30=100).

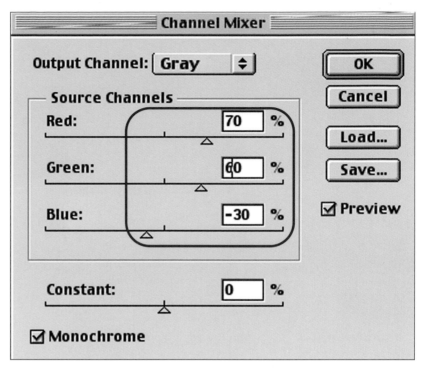

Image 33

Image 34

5. The resulting image (Image 34) is significantly better than the straight conversion (Image 31). It could still use a little overall refinement to the contrast, but the blues in the image are a much better representation of the actual scene. To finish the conversion, a simple refinement could be made using the curves, as shown on pages 57–59.

If you will be printing your image on a device that allows you to use more than one ink, you can make your black & white image look even better by actually printing it in color. Using two or more inks allows you to create a much richer black, and a fuller range of midtones. An example is shown in Images 35 and 36.

Image 35
(Printed with black ink only)

Image 36
(Printed with four inks)

1. Convert the grayscale image back to a color mode (Image>Mode>RGB or CMYK). CMYK is used for professional printing, but RGB will work fine with many home printers.

2. When you have completed the conversion, run your eyedropper tool over the image and look at the info panel (Window> Show Info). You should see a percentage of color used in each color channel of the photo (Image 37). Each channel represents one ink (in the CMYK mode), so you can tell that the image will print with four inks. You can also convert to the RGB mode when printing on your own equipment. The info window will then show the RGB information in addition to the CMYK.

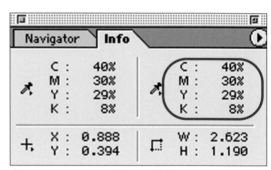

Image 37

3. The one pitfall to watch out for is potential color shifts—often a slightly bluish. If you are printing the image with your own equipment, you can experiment with using the curves to slightly reduce the blue in the image, or (if your printer software allows) try adjusting down the blue in the printout. If you are working with a professional printer, talk with them about this issue before submitting your work to be printed.

Duotone Mode

For professional printing, you may also want to consider using the duotone mode (printing a black & white image with two inks). This usually saves a bit of money on professional jobs and creates a very nice look. Consult your professional printer for costs and options.

LITHOGRAPHIC FILM (POSTERIZATION)

▶ Overview

Posterization is a term used to describe the reduction of the full range of gray tones in a black & white to pure black and white only. The resulting images have a very strong graphic quality, but very little detail.

In a traditional darkroom, posterization involves the use of lithographic film. This film, which is designed for offset printing, produces an image consisting of only black & white areas with no intermediate gray tones. Making a positive print requires making an enlarged transparency on lith film (this will be a positive), contact printing that transparency to a second sheet of lith film (to make a negative), then printing from the new negative to make a positive on photographic paper. Since this is a contact-printing process, the size of the negative will determine the final print size, and new negatives must be produced if more than one print size is required.

Suffice it to say that Photoshop makes the job a lot easier. There are two basic techniques for achieving the desired result. These are covered below. Immediately following the techniques, you will find some helpful information for optimizing your results.

▶ Techniques

Posterization Function

1. Begin with an image in the grayscale mode (Image 1).

2. Go to Image>Adjust>Posterize.

3. If you like, adjust the number of grays in the image, using the levels box within the posterize dialogue box. Setting it at two will produce an image of pure black & white. Any setting up to about five or ten will produce a relatively dramatic result. Images 2–4 show the effects of a few different settings.

Image 1
(original image by Jeff Smith)

Image 2	*Image 3*	*Image 4*
(posterization with two levels)	*(posterization with three levels)*	*(posterization with four levels)*

Brightness/Contrast Function

1. Start with an image in the grayscale mode (Image 1).

2. Adjust the contrast (Image>Adjust>Brightness/Contrast) to a very high number. Selecting +100 will produce an image made up of black and white only (Image 5). Using this method at lesser intensities (less than +100) produces a slightly different look than the Posterize command (Image 6).

While +100 contrast creates essentially the same look, you can see there are differences between it and a two-level posterization. The shadow under the model's chin is different, as are the model's right arm and the rocks behind her. The result of adding a few gray tones with the brightness/contrast dialogue box (say, reducing the contrast to +90) also produces a smoother, more photographic look than adding a few gray tones with the posterize command. Use whichever method produces the result you want.

Image 5	*Image 6*
(contrast +100)	*(contrast +90)*

Levels Function

As you can tell, there is almost always more than one way to do something in Photoshop. The one you choose depends on the look you want.

1. Start with an image in the grayscale mode (Image 1).

2. To create a posterization effect with levels, simple move the triangular black and white sliders in close to the middle of the histogram (Image 7). The closer they are to the center, the more compressed the tonal range becomes (i.e., the closer to pure black & white tones only) (Image 8).

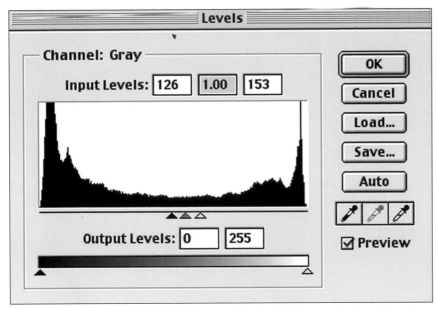

Image 7

Image 8

Posterization with Curves

This method produces results very similar to those achieved using method three, but might offer a bit more control.

1. Begin with an image in the grayscale mode (Image 1).

2. Open the curves dialogue box (Image>Adjust>Curves).

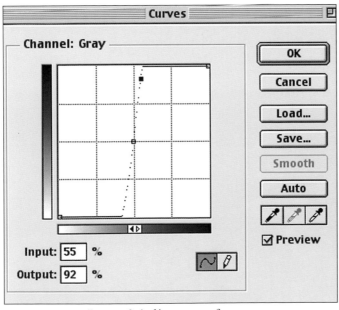

*Image 9 (adjustment of curves
for posterization effect)*

*Image 10 (resulting image
from these settings)*

3. Click to place a point at the middle of the line and nail down the midtone range.

4. Click to place a point about halfway between the midpoint and either the black or white endpoint.

5. If you clicked near the black point, drag it up to the very top of the grid box (Image 9). If you clicked near the white point, drag it down to the very bottom on the grid box.

6. As you drag the line, the diagonal running through the center gets steeper, showing that the tonal range is being compressed (data that used to span many shades of gray, now spans only a very few). Wherever the curve becomes a flat line pressed against the top or bottom of the grid box, you have compressed the tonal range into pure black or pure white.

▶ Hints and Tips

If there are people in the photo to be posterized, make sure their overall skin tone is one of the lightest areas of the image to ensure that it reproduces as clean white. Images 11 and 12 show a nice portrait, but a bad choice for posterization (unless you are going for a very unusual look).

Select photographs to posterize that are highly graphic and don't need detail to be appreciated. All texture and fine detail will be destroyed in the posterized version of the image. Image 13 is a nice portrait, but a bad candidate for posterization (Image 14).

For an interesting effect, try posterizing a color image. You'll find some very interesting color shifts that might be quite to your liking. Image 13 was converted using the posterize command with four levels—the results are shown in Image 15.

Image 11
(original image by Jeff Smith)

Image 12
(image converted to grayscale and posterized)

Image 13
(original image by Jeff Smith)

Image 14

Image 15

Image 16
(unaltered grayscale image)

Image 17
(customized grayscale image)

Image 18
(Image 16 posterized
with +90 contrast)

Image 19
(Image 17 posterized
with +90 contrast)

If you posterize an image and aren't happy with the result, making the original image darker or lighter can often improve the posterization. Also consider dodging/burning areas of the original image to help you control what goes black and what goes white in the posterization. In Image 17, textured areas were burned in on the side of the model's blouse (to keep better detail), and her right arm was dodged to keep it from going black. The entire image was also slightly brightened by lightening the midtones using the levels.

TECHNIQUE 9
ORTHOCHROMATIC FILM

● ●

▶ Overview

Like panchromatic black and white film, orthochromatic film (used primarily for copy and graphic arts work) is most strongly sensitive to blue, green, and yellow light. In prints made from it, these tones will be rendered as relatively light. Unlike panchromatic, however, orthochromatic film does not respond to red

Image 1

Image 2

light at all. As a result, these tones will be rendered as dark in the print.

To reproduce the effect then, it is necessary to lighten the blues tones and darken the reds. This can be accomplished using the channel mixer.

▶ Technique

1. Begin with a color image in the RGB mode. The effect will be most dramatic if your image contains relatively strong blues/greens and reds (Image 1).

2. Open the channel mixer (Image>Adjust>Channel Mixer). Activate the monochrome box at the bottom of the dialogue box. To darken the reds and lighten the blues and greens, set the controls to somewhere in the neighborhood of Red=-110, Blue=+105, Green=+105 (Image 3).

Image 2 shows the straight conversion to grayscale (roughly how unfiltered panchromatic film would show the scene). Image 4 shows the result of using the channel mixer to create an effect like that of orthochromatic film.

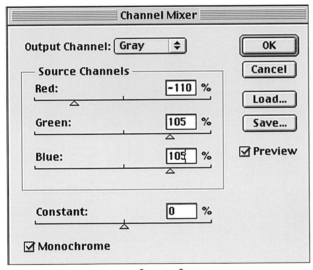

Image 3

Quick Tip

To maintain the overall brightness and contrast of your image, make sure that the settings of the three controls add up to a total of +100 (as shown above).

Image 4

TECHNIQUE 10
LENS FLARE

● ●

▶ Overview

Lens flare occurs when unwanted light (usually from a direct, intense source such as the sun) enters the camera lens. This light causes loss of contrast. As the light reflects off the aperture blades, however, it also causes bright featureless highlights (or a series of bright geometric shapes). These effects are traditionally considered bad, and are usually avoided by using a lens shade (or camera angle) to prevent unwanted light from entering the

This light causes loss of contrast.

Image 1

lens. In some instances, however, flare can be used creatively to enhance composition, or suggest glaringly bright conditions to the viewer.

Photoshop offers a filter that, while not 100% satisfactory, can provide the appearance of flare where needed.

▶ Technique

1. Begin with an image in the RGB mode. Selecting one where the angle of the light is clear is helpful for creating the most realistic effect (Image 1).

2. You may find it useful to increase the canvas size of your image by three to four inches in each direction (Image>Canvas Size) (Image 2). In the next step you will be applying the lens fare filter. This will require you to position a light source on your image, and will result in dramatically reduced contrast around that spot. Having a couple extra inches of canvas will allow you to position the light source off the edge of your image, leaving the contrast less degraded in the original image. When you've completed fine-tuning the effect, you can simply crop the image back to its original dimensions.

3. Open the lens flare dialogue box (Filter>Render>Lens Flare) (Image 3). A cursor will appear (denoting the light source), which you can move with your mouse to the appropriate location

> You may find it useful to increase the canvas size of your image . . .

Image 2

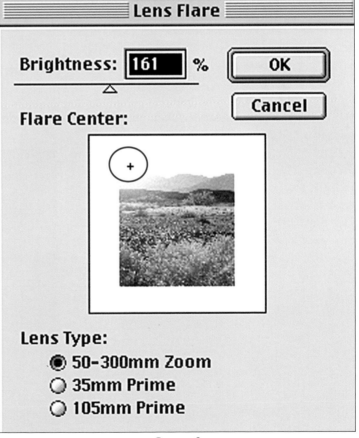

Image 3

Image 4

Image 5

in the image. Carefully evaluating the original image will help you decide the most logical place for the placement of this light source. You can also select the lens type for the effect you want, as well as the overall brightness. Experiment with a few combinations. When you've settled on an effect you like, click OK to initiate the change (Image 4).

4. Once you've clicked OK and the filter has run, you can also reduce the intensity of the effect that is achieved by going to Edit>Fade Lens Flare (Image 6). This can be helpful for restoringa little detail to the light source area, where it may have been lost (Image 5). For some very interesting effects, you may also want to experiment with adjusting the layer modes (Layer>Layer Style> Blending Options) (Image 7 shows the difference mode).

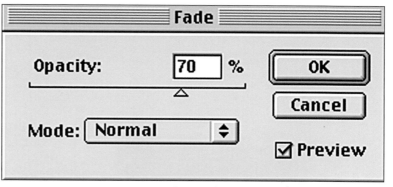

Image 6

Image 7

TECHNIQUE 11
NEUTRAL DENSITY FILTERS

▶ Overview

Neutral density (ND) filters are used by photographers to reduce the amount of light entering the camera in situations where the desired aperture/shutter speed combination would otherwise yield an overexposed image. Unlike polarizing or other filters, ND filters do not affect the color or quality of the light entering the camera, merely the amount of light.

Regular ND filters contain an equal amount of density across the entire filter (reducing the exposure equally throughout the frame). Graduated ND filters provide greater density across half of the filter, fading to little or no density on the other half. These filters are especially useful for landscape photographers who frequently encounter scenes with bright elements in one part of the frame (such as the sky or a distant mountain), and dark elements in another (such as dark trees in the foreground). Using a graduated ND filter in these situations helps to control contrast when the difference in brightness between the highlights and the shadows exceeds the film's exposure latitude.

However, filters and adapters can be cumbersome, and often you may simply not have the filter in place when the right moment occurs. Fortunately, Photoshop can help to rescue an otherwise ruined image. In addition, because you can select precisely where density needs to be increased, your control over the image is actually increased dramatically.

▶ Technique

1. Begin with an image in the RGB mode. It should be noted that, while this technique will help to increase density in overexposed areas, it will not be of use in areas that are pure white or black. If your image is so badly exposed that you believe extreme adjustments will be required to produce an acceptable image, you will probably be disappointed. Better candidates for this technique are images with small to moderate exposure problems (Image 1).

. . . filters and adapters can be cumbersome . . .

Image 1

Next, select the individual areas to be altered.

2. Next, select the individual areas to be altered. You can use the magic wand, marquee, lasso—or any other selection tool you feel is appropriate. In this case the image needs to be divided into three areas: the dark foreground, the bright background, and the more correctly exposed midground. As you make each selection, save it (Select>Save Selection), since you may want to use it again. To blur the edges of each selection for better blending, use the Feather command (Selection>Feather) set to two pixels. Using the selections, copy and paste each selected area to a new level

Image 2

Image 3

Image 4

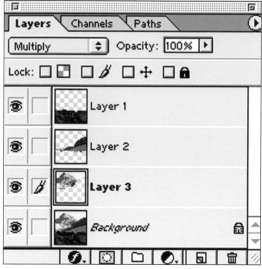

Image 5

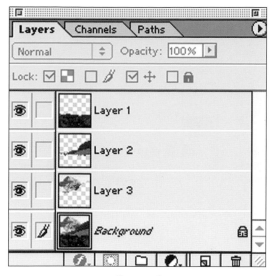

Image 6

(Images 2, 3, 4). (The background should remain your original photograph, as in Image 5.)

3. In the layers palette, activate the layer containing the overexposed part of the image by clicking on it. Next, we will need to adjust the layer mode, which controls blending (the way the pixels on one layer interact with the pixels in other layers). When the layer mode is set to normal, the pixels do not react at all. When it is set to multiply, the color values of the layer are multiplied by the one beneath it. In this case, setting the layer mode to multiply (Image 6) allows us to add density and saturation to an area of the photograph (Image 7).

Image 7

4. If the effect is too dramatic, you can reduce the density of the layer by setting the opacity to less than 100%. In Image 8, the opacity was reduced to 80%.

Image 8

5. Next, activate the layer containing the area of the image that is underexposed. Set the layer mode to "screen" (Image 9) in order to lighten this area of the image (Image 10). Adjust the opacity of the layer to achieve the desired result.

6. Your image should be looking a lot better, but if fine tuning still needs to be done, you can adjust the curves, levels, or brightness/contrast for each layer until you are satisfied. If you prefer to flatten the image first, you can load the appropriate saved selection (Select>Load Selection) and make the same adjustments. In this case, adjusting the color balance in the foreground helped to remove some of the bluish color cast, and to improve the local contrast (Image 11).

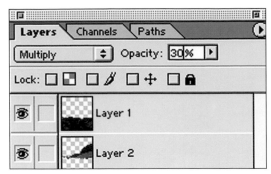

Image 9

Image 10

Image 11

Quick Tip

You aren't limited to one layer to build density. In the above image, the sky area was reselected and copied into a new layer (set to multiply) to build additional color in this very pale area. Since the color was also very flat, the new sky layer was duplicated. Using the Filter>Render>Difference Clouds command on this duplicate layer added some texture. The "cloud" layer was then set to the overlay layer mode so it would blend seamlessly with the underlying layers. Its opacity was set quite low (about 30%) to add just a hint of texture. Look carefully at Image 11 to see the results.

TECHNIQUE 12
SOFT FOCUS

▶ Overview

Soft focus is typically used in portraits (most often of women) to create a softer, more flattering effect. With today's high-resolution films, a little softening can help to hide the little flaws that most people don't want to see in a portrait. Soft focus isn't limited to portraiture, of course; it may be appropriate for adding a dreamy quality to just about anything.

Two warnings should be kept in mind, however. First, soft focus should not be used to the extent that the image seems blurry or out of focus. Soft focus images should be acceptably sharp, but with a softening of hard lines. Second, soft focus can easily be overused and look like a gimmick. It's not appropriate for all (or even most) images. Use it selectively when it contributes to the success of a particular image.

Soft focus is normally achieved using either a special soft focus lens, or soft focus filters attached to a regular lens. With Photoshop, you can achieve much more precise control, and apply the soft focus look as selectively as you like.

▶ Technique

1. Begin with an image in the RGB or grayscale mode (Image 1).

Image 1 (original image by Rick Ferro)

2. Apply a Gaussian blur to the entire image (Filter>Blur> Gaussian Blur). Ten pixels is a good starting point (Image 2). If this or another number gives you a look you are happy with, you can stop right here (Image 3). More often (especially with portraits, where sharpness is especially desirable in the eyes), you will want to apply the effect more selectively. If so, proceed to the next step.

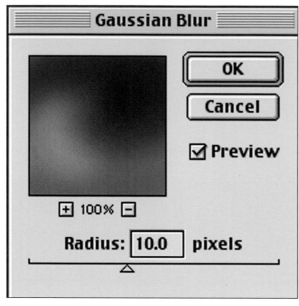

Image 2

Image 3

3. In the history palette, click on the box to activate the history brush icon next to the Gaussian blur history (Image 4). Then click on the "open" stage in the history palette. The blue will disappear, but the Gaussian blur stage will remain visible in the history palette.

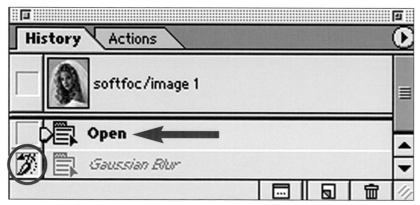

Image 4

4. Select the history brush and set it to the lighten mode in the history brush options menu. This will allow the brush only to blur dark into light, for a more subtle effect. Set the opacity of the history brush to 50% to start.

5. Select a soft brush (double click on the brush and set the hardness to 0 if necessary). Next, simply "paint" on the soft focus

effect wherever you want it. Image 5 shows an unsoftened area of this portrait. Image 6 shows that same area with softness painted on from the Gaussian blur history stage. Image 7 shows the completed portrait.

Image 5

Image 6

Image 7

▶ **Variations**

Selective Softness

If you want an equal degree of softness across the entire image (i.e., you don't need to control precise degrees of softness in specific locations), try the following method.

1. Begin with an image in the RGB or grayscale mode.

2. Duplicate the background image (Layer>Duplicate Layer). Click on the new layer in the layers palette to activate it (Image 8).

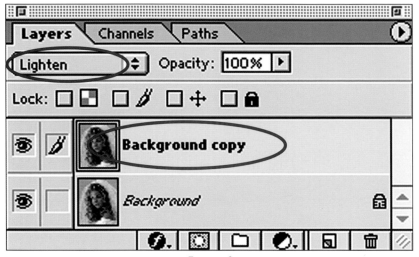

Image 8

3. Apply a Gaussian blur to the new layer (see pg. 78, Image 2).

4. In the layers palette, set the layer mode of the duplicate layer to lighten.

5. Since this effect is on a separate layer, you can adjust the layer opacity to reduce the softness as needed.

This effect is also useful if you want to apply equal softness to all but a very small part of the image. In that case, follow steps one through five, then select the eraser tool and use the eraser tool options menu to set its opacity to about 50%. Next, simply "erase" the areas in the duplicate layer where less softness is desired.

Clear Center Soft Focus

Clear center soft focus filters are also popular. These provide softening at the edges of the image, but not in the center. To duplicate the effect, turn to page 35 and follow steps 1–5 for vignetting. With your selection active, copy the selected area and paste it into a new layer. Next, apply a Gaussian blur to the new layer and set the new layer's mode to lighten. You can also adjust the layer opacity as you like.

. . . apply equal softness to all but a very small part of the image.

TECHNIQUE 13
CORRECTING
VERTICAL DISTORTIONS

► **Overview**

When we look up to see the long vertical lines of a building, we perceive them as converging toward the top of the structure. The same thing happens when we tilt our cameras up. Sometimes this distortion can help us to create interesting compositions. More often, it is quite distracting. This common technical flaw can be easily rectified with Photoshop.

► **Technique**

1. Begin with a digital image in any color mode (Image 1). The dimensions of your final image will likely shift slightly during this

The same thing happens when we tilt our cameras up.

Image 1

operation, so you may wish to start with an image that has somewhat more pixels (either in resolution or dimensions) than you need in your final image. This will give you room to resize it without losing any sharpness.

2. You may wish to use guides to help you get the verticals perfectly straight. If so, with the rulers showing (View>Show Rulers), drag vertical guides onto your image.

3. Select the entire image (Select>All).

4. Next, use Edit>Transform to correct the verticals. Selecting either the perspective or the distort control (under Edit>Transform) will do the job. Simply click on one of the corners of the image and drag it in or out to correct the distortion. Whatever changes you make should be mirrored left to right (Image 2). With the perspective control this will happen automatically; with the distort control, you will have to make the change to each side yourself.

Image 2

5. When you are pleased with the results, hit enter to apply the change. Then click outside the selected area to deactivate it.

6. Finally, use the cropping tool to remove any of the white background that has been revealed during the procedure (Image 3).

Image 3

RED-EYE REDUCTION

▶ **Overview**

Red-eye occurs when the camera and light source (usually an on-camera flash) are directly in line with the subject's eyes. This is mostly a problem with point-and-shoot cameras, but it can be easily corrected in Photoshop whenever it occurs.

▶ **Technique**

1. Begin with an image in the RGB mode (Image 1).

... it can be easily corrected in Photoshop whenever it occurs.

Image 1

2. Use the magnifying glass to zoom in tightly on the area to be corrected (Image 2).

3. Create a new layer (Layer>New>Layer) and set it to the color mode (Image 3).

Image 2

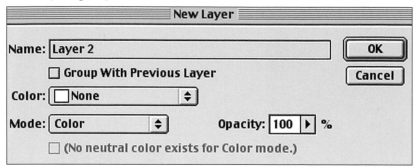

Image 3

4. Double click on the foreground color swatch to open the color picker, and select a color close to the subject's actual eye color. (How close you need to be to create realistic results depends on the prominence of the eyes in the photo. Here they are small, so a close approximation will work—and almost anything will be better than red!)

5. Select a tool to apply the new color (paintbrush, airbrush, etc.) and paint the color onto the new layer to cover the areas affected by red-eye (Image 4). This is the same technique used for handcoloring, but it is used here correctively.

6. Zoom out. If the image looks better, you're done (Image 5). If you need to refine the effect, you can zoom back in.

Image 4

Image 5

TECHNIQUE 15
CREATING CUSTOM BORDERS

Custom borders
can add a nice
finishing touch to
many photographs.

▶ **Overview**

Custom borders, while not appropriate for every image, can add a nice finishing touch to many photographs. Often, they can also help to define or improve the composition. While a traditional custom printer can use overlays and other tools to create beautiful borders, their services are often prohibitively expensive. When creating borders with Photoshop, you have more choices and more control.

▶ **Techniques**

In the following sections, we will work through a few basic techniques for adding borders. Once you have learned these, you will probably want to experiment with your own variations to develop your own special looks and styles.

Simple Keyline

In this section, you will learn to apply a simple border (using black or whatever color you choose). This is a very effective addition to an image with very light areas at the edges, since it helps to define the border of the frame and keep the viewer's eye on the subject.

Quick Tip

In this lesson, you'll learn how to create custom borders using the tools that come packaged with Photoshop (and your scanner). If you decide you really like custom borders and will be using them frequently, you may want to consider investing in a plug-in (software that runs within Photoshop and adds a new function to it). Plug-ins that can be used to create dozens of custom borders are widely available in software catalogs or on the Internet.

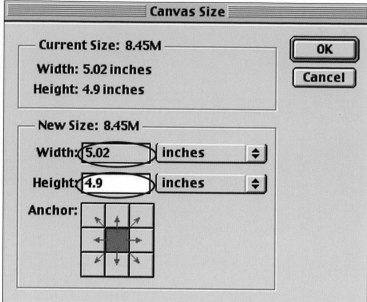

Image 1 (Original image by Rick Ferro)   *Image 2*

1. Begin with an image in any color mode. If you select the grayscale modc, you will only be able to add a border in black or shades of gray (Image 1).

2. Select the color you want your border to be by setting the background color. To do this, double click on the background color swatch near the bottom of the tools palette. Doing this will open the color picker, and allow you to select a color.

3. With the background color properly selected, go to Image> Canvas Size (Image 2).

4. To add a simple border, all you need to do is slightly increase the width and height of the canvas. This will create an area around your image that is filled in with the background color you selected in step 2.

To add a relatively fine border, try increasing the canvas size by .05". In this case, that would mean increasing the width to 5.07" and the height to 4.95" (Image 3).

To add a sturdier border, try increasing the canvas size by .1". In this case, that would mean increasing the width to 5.12" and the height to 5.0" (Image 4).

5. Don't forget, there is no reason you can't add a border in color if you like (Images 5–10). For the most effective look, try using colors for the frame that are present in the image. You can select a color from the image as your background color by following the instructions in step 2. With the color picker open, click on the color in the image that you want to use. This will become your background color. In Images 5–10, tones from the photograph were used to create the borders.

Image 3

Image 4

Image 5

Image 6

Image 7

Image 8

Image 9

Image 10

Stylized Vignette Border

In this section, you'll learn to create a border that's really a combination of a stylized vignette and a border. It's a nice device to consider when you have areas around the subject (like a distracting background) that you'd like to conceal without cropping the image.

1. Begin with an image in any color mode (Image 11). If you select the grayscale mode, you will only be able to add enhancements in black or shades of gray. Since you will be applying filters, you may wish to work in the RGB mode, since this will offer the most possibilities (not all filters work in the other color modes).

Image 11 (original photo by Rick Ferro)

Image 12

2. Select the area that will not be affected by the border (you can use the marquee tool, magic wand, lasso—whatever you like). Save the selection (Select>Save Selection), naming it whatever you like (I chose "vignette," as you can see in Image 13). Then, go back to your image and use the Select>Inverse command to invert the selection (Image 12).

3. With the selection active, copy and paste the selected area into a new layer. (If copying and pasting does not create a new layer automatically, you can create a new layer [Layer>New>Layer] and activate it in the layers palette to paste onto it.)

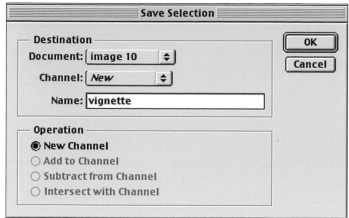

Image 13

Image 14

4. Click on the new layer in the layers palette to activate it. (Image 14).

5. With the new layer activated, try running a few different filters on it, or changing the layer mode until you have an effect you like. For Image 15, I used the watercolor filter plus a moderate amount of noise, then set the layer mode to multiply (to darken the layer).

Image 15

6. If you like the effect, you can stop (in which case, you've created more a vignette than a border). Personally, I think it needs a finishing touch.

7. Go to Select>Load Selection, and load the selection you made in step 2 of this project.

8. Our goal will be to add a fine line of color to provide definition between the central area of the photo and the border area. Begin by setting your foreground color to the color you want this border to be (white or black are good starting points).

9. Create a new layer if you wish. If you do not, the line will be created on whichever layer is active when you perform step 10.

10. With the selection still active, go to Edit>Stroke and enter a value for the width of the line you want (Image 16). Three pixels will create a fine line, but you can go as high as you like, depending on the effect you want to achieve. You'll probably want to leave the stroke centered (to ensure it covers the transition area between unaltered photo and border). If you are creating the stroke on a new layer, you do not need to worry about setting blending in this box, as you'll be able to do it in the layers palette. If you are creating the stroke directly on your image, you may want to experiment with the settings here (you can always use the history palette to undo anything you don't like).

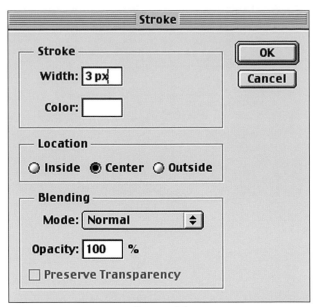

Image 16

11. For this photo (Image 17), a three-pixel white line was added (with the opacity at 100% and the mode as normal).

There are thousands of possible variations on this idea—don't be afraid to experiment. After all, half the fun of doing a border this way is that you can try out all your ideas without having to wait for (or pay for) custom printing work.

Textured Edges

Textured edges can add a little life to a photograph. Using the filters in Photoshop, it's easy to experiment with many different styles of edges, and decide which one might add that important finishing touch to your image. Although the effects you can create are limited only by your imagination, a single, relatively simple process using alpha channel selections can be used to create them all.

1. Begin with an image in the RGB or grayscale mode. This will give you the greatest number of filters to choose from (some filters are not available in other color modes). This image should be cropped as you would like it to appear in the final version (Image 18).

2. If it is not already, set white as the background color (using the color swatches near the bottom of the tools palette).

3. Increase the canvas size (not image size) of your image (Image>Canvas Size). About an inch in each direction should do

Image 17

Image 18
(original photo by Rick Ferro)

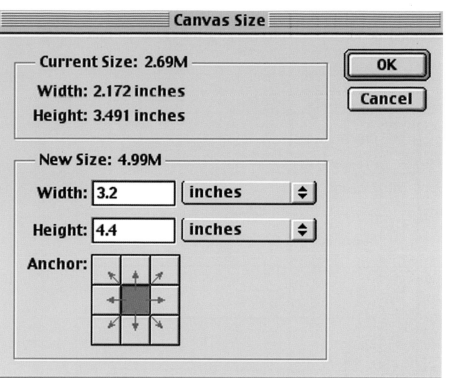

Image 19

the trick (in the example shown in Image 19, the canvas size was increased from 2.2" to 3.2" in width, and from 3.4" to 4.4" in height). Creating this extra space around the photo will give you the access to the edges of the frame that will be required to create uneven edge effects.

4. Use the rectangular marquee tool to select the perimeter of your image. Next, invert the selection (Select>Inverse).

5. With this selection still active, go to Select>Save Selection and create a new channel. Since this example will show how to create the effect of torn edges, that was the name selected for the new channel (Image 20).

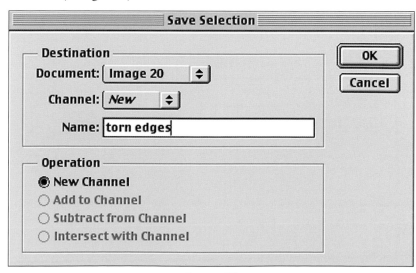

Image 20

6. Once you have saved your selection (called an alpha channel selection), go to the channels palette and click on the new channel (Image 21).

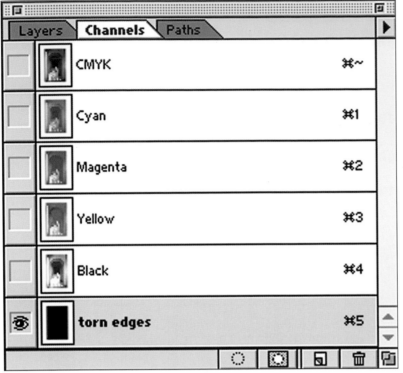

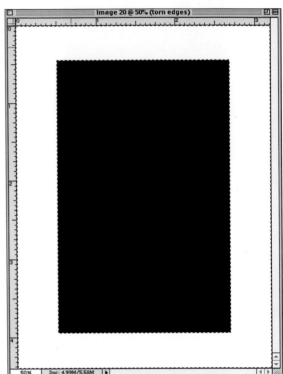

Image 21

Image 22

Clicking on the new channel in the channels palette will bring up the channel in your main window. The selected area will be white, and the unselected area will be black.

7. The selection should still be active on the white area (indicated by the dancing dotted line around it). The next step is to expand that selected area slightly into the edges of the black area (which denoted the actual edges of the photograph). To do this, go to Select>Modify>Expand. You can enter whatever value you like. Somewhere in the neighborhood of ten to sixteen pixels is a good starting point (Image 23).

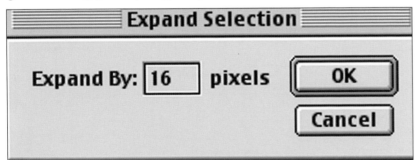

Image 23

8. Returning to the main window, the active selection on the new channel should now have expanded to include both white *and* black portions of the channel.

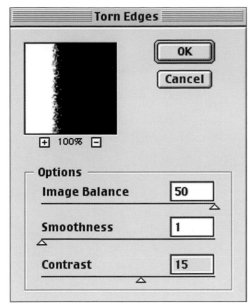

Image 24

Image 26

Now you can get creative. For this example, we'll create the look of torn edges, but several other variations are also shown at the end of this section.

9. With the selection still active, go to Filter>Sketch>Torn Edges. Adjust the settings as you like, and apply the filter (Image 24).

10. Return to the layers palette and click on the layer containing your image to activate it.

11. Load the new selection, by going to Select>Load Selection and choosing the "torn edges" channel (Image 25).

12. With the new selection active, go to Edit>Clear to clear the selected area and create the look of torn edges. Deactivate the selection (by clicking on the image with the marquee tool) to see the results (Image 26).

There are a wide number of possible variations that can be applied using this method. You may want to try applying more than one filter in step 9, or perhaps multiple different filters. You may want to blur the selection or add grain to it.

On the next page you'll see examples and brief descriptions of a few of the possible combinations. Each of the filter combinations discussed can replace step 9 in this procedure and create a totally different look.

In this example, a halftone pattern was created around the border of the image. In step 9 of the previously described procedure, simply use the color halftone filter (Filter>Pixelate>Color Halftone) to achieve this result.

In this example, the border was created using the crosshatch filter. In step 9 of the previously described procedure, simply apply this filter (Filter>Brush Strokes>Crosshatch) to achieve this result. For the most dramatic results, set the stroke length, sharpness, and strength to their highest settings.

In this example, the border was created using two filters. In step 9 of the previously described procedure, the ripple filter (Filter>Distort>Ripple) was applied. The same filter was then applied a second time using slightly different settings. Finally, the wave filter was applied (Filter>Distort>Wave), to create a slightly more complex pattern.

In this example, the border was created using two filters. In step 9 of the previously described procedure, the crystallize filter (Filter>Pixelate>Crystallize) was applied. Next, the charcoal filter was applied (Filter>Sketch>Charcoal), to outline the edges of the crystallized cells and create this lattice-like look on the borders of the image.

Quick Tip

This same technique can be used to create the look of a Polaroid transfer—just start with a Polaroid transfer border and use all the same steps!

Image 31

Image 32

Composite Borders

In this section, you will learn how to use your scanner to create and apply borders. If you like this technique, you may want to keep a file of your favorites on your hard drive to apply to images again and again.

1. To begin, select your border. This could be a traditional ragged black border like the one created by using a filed-out negative holder to print your negative, or it could be something else—a textile, newsprint, another photo, etc. Whatever it is, find a scannable sample.

2. Decide on the highest resolution and largest size you think you'll need. If you routinely print 8"x10"s or larger, scan it to produce an image of that size and at the resolution your printer requires for the quality of print you like. If you decide to use the border on a smaller photo, you can always reduce its size. If you are sure you'll never use the border again, you can scan it at whatever size you need for this photo.

3. Scan your border. In this case, a photo with a rough black border (printed in a traditional black & white darkroom) was used (Image 31).

4. In this example, the area that was to be the border (the black area) was well defined. As you can see, it has an irregular edge on both the inner and outer perimeter. Because this needed to be preserved, it made sense to set the border up so that it could be placed *over* a photograph (placing the photo over the border would have covered those interesting irregular edges). Therefore, the border was copied to its own layer (Layer>Duplicate Layer).

5. Using the eyedropper tool, make sure that the white area in the center (where the image will show through) is pure white. When you place the eyedropper tool over the area, the info palette (Window>Show Info) should read 0% in the C, M, Y, and K fields for CMYK, 255 in R, G, and B fields for RGB, or 0% in the K field for grayscale. If it does not, select the area and fill it with 100% white (Edit>Fill). It is important that this area be pure white because we are going to change the layer mode to multiply, and any color information in this area will affect the look of the photo we place under it.

6. In the layers palette, set the mode of the layer with the border on it to multiply.

7. Next, select the photograph to which you will apply the border, making sure that the border is close in size to (or bigger than) the scan of the photograph that you will use (Image 32).

8. Open your digital file of the photograph, select the entire image, and copy it (Edit>Copy).

9. Return to the image of the border and paste the photo into this document (Edit>Paste). If it does not paste into a new level automatically, you can undo the operation (Edit>Undo), create a new layer (Layer>New>Layer) and paste the photo onto that.

10. When you have done this, your layers palette should show at least two layers (one for the photo and one for the border). If you have set your border up as described in step 4 (so the image will be placed behind the border), you will have three layers (one for the photo, one for the border, and a background layer) (Image 33). (Remember, if you'll be placing your photo behind the border, the layer with the photo on it must be lower on the layers palette than the layer with the border on it. If it is not, simply click on the photo layer and drag it to a position lower than the border layer.)

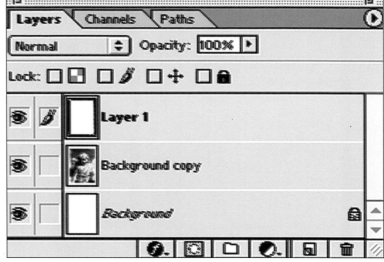

Image 33

11. With the pieces in place, all that is left to do is to adjust the border to fit the image. To do this, click on the layer containing the border in the layers palette.

12. To adjust the border, go to Image> Transform>Distort. A black line with box-shaped handles will appear. Use your mouse to

Image 34

Image 35

click and drag these handles one by one until the border fits the image as you want it to (Image 34).

13. The image is complete (Image 35). You may wish to flatten and save it at this point, but consider saving a copy of the unflattened image in case you ever want to make an adjustment (or use another border).

This basic technique has limitless applications. A few variations are shown below.

Foliage was scanned, and noise added to it, to create the border. A white keyline was inserted by selecting the original photograph and adding a two-point white stroke (Edit>Stroke).

Text was scanned. The layer containing the scanned text was copied twice. The copied layers were set to 50% opacity, then rotated 90° and 180° to create a crisscross pattern.

Crushed red velvet was scanned, and a four-pixel Gaussian blur added to it. A black keyline was inserted by selecting the original photograph and adding a five-point stroke (Edit>Stroke).

Lumber was scanned with the grain running across the frame at about a 45° angle. Aside from slight color correction, the scan was used without any alteration.

TECHNIQUE 16
PAINTING WITH LIGHT

► Overview

Light painting is a technique which allows one or more small light sources to be moved precisely over the subject during a long (or multiple) exposure of the frame. The technique can produce a unique special effect, or be used as a tool for very precise lighting, especially of products (since these hold still for long exposures better than people do). It's a time-consuming, but very interesting technique.

► Technique

1. Begin with an image in any color mode (Image 1).

2. In the history palette, make sure that the history brush icon is placed directly next to the version of the image you want to work with. This could be the original image (at the very top of the history palette), or it might be the image as it occurs a few steps down the histories. In this example, the raw scan was color balanced and cleaned up after scanning. Since we want to work with the final, color balanced image (not the raw scan), the history brush icon was moved down to the last step in the history palette (Image 2).

3. Go to Edit>Fill. Select Black and 100% opacity to fill the entire image. At this point the entire frame should

Image 1

Quick Tip

Note that, although this technique simulates light painting, it cannot put light in places where there were shadows in the original image. If you are concerned about achieving the most controlled results, start with an image with even overall lighting and thin, open shadows.

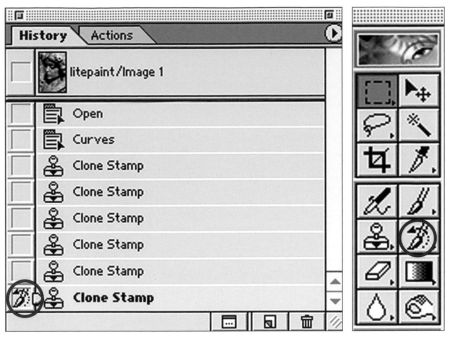

Image 2 Image 3

Image 4

be black. The photo is still there though, preserved and accessible via the history brush. Think of the photograph as your subject, sitting in place and waiting for you to shine light on it to make it visible. The "light" for this light-painting technique will be the history brush.

4. Select the history brush from the tools palette (Image 3). Then select a brush size from the brushes menu at the top of the screen. You'll probably want to start with a relatively large, soft brush (especially if you don't have an extremely steady hand and/or a degree in fine art). If you have a graphics tablet, this would be a great place to use it.

5. Next, turn to the options menu for the history brush. By controlling the opacity of the history brush, you can essentially control the exposure. Set the opacity to 100% for correct exposure, or to a lower number to—in essence—underexpose the image.

You can also select from a number of modes for the history brush by accessing the pull-down option menu at the top of the screen. Experiment with these modes and see which ones create looks that you like. Image 4 was created using two large brushes, both in the lighten mode, one set to 100% opacity and the other set to 80% opacity.

If you are slightly less daring about doing the painting yourself, try this variation.

1. Begin with an image in the RGB mode.

2. Create a new layer (Layer>New>Layer) and fill it with black (Edit>Fill).

3. Select the eraser tool, and a large, soft brush. Set the opacity to 80–100%. Erase random lines evenly across the entire image (leaving plenty of black).

4. Go to work with the filters to distort the black layer (which is now full of eraser holes). Try the ripple or wave filters (Filter>Distort>Wave *or* Ripple) and experiment with different settings. You may also want to blur the layer considerably in order to soften and blur the edges of the erased areas (Filter> Blur>Gaussian Blur).

Image 5 was created using this method. While it does not offer the precise control of the first method discussed, that may not be a bad thing—sometimes you can achieve surprisingly interesting results you might never have envisioned otherwise.

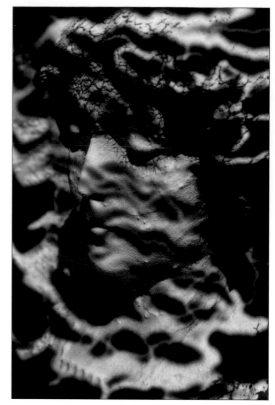

Image 5

Quick Tip

The incredible freedom we have when working with digital images also comes with some perils akin to those experienced behind the camera. One of these is controlling contrast. If you've worked with digital images much, you've experienced how easy it can be to get your shadows just right only to find your highlights totally devoid of detail, or to finally get the right red on the model's dress only to notice that the sky has become purple. In these cases, the history brush can be a lifesaver.

Like light painting, the history brush can be used to make very small, precise alterations in the image. Using the example given above of the model's dress, you can get the right red on the dress, mark that as the source for the history brush (by putting the history brush icon next to that stage in the history palette), then go back to a version of the image where the sky was right and use the history brush to "paint" the desired red back onto the dress.

The same technique can be used to open up stubborn shadows. Simply get the highlights right, mark that step in the history palette with the history brush, then get the shadows right and use the history brush to paint the highlights (or midtones) back in.

TECHNIQUE 17
CROSS PROCESSING

▶ Overview

Cross processing means developing film in chemistry other than that which it was designed to be processed in (most often E-6 film processed in C-41 chemistry, or C-41 film processed in E-6 chemistry). The process creates interesting (and somewhat unpredictable) color shifts that vary with the film, its exposure, the chemistry, and the development process. The following process simulates the cross processed look of Kodak VHC, with pinkish-yellow highlights, and bluish shadows.

▶ Technique

1. Begin with an image in the RGB mode. This image should have good contrast and be color balanced accurately. With portraits, you'll have the best results with skin tones that are quite light (Image 1). Images with lighter tones overall also tend to work better than darker images.

2. Create a new adjustment layer set to curves. To do this, go to Layer>New Adjustment Layer>Curves (Image 2).

3. When you click OK in the dialogue box for the adjustment layer, the curves box will appear. Select the

Image 1 (original image by Jeff Smith)

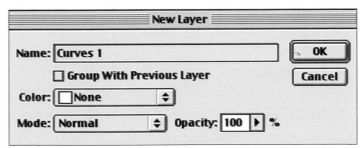

Image 2

blue channel from the pull-down menu at the top of the box (Image 3). Move the highlight point down as shown in Image 3. You can finetune this setting (and all the following ones) as you like. Here, it was set to Input: 255, Output: 190. Click in the center of the curve to add a point in the midtones. Pull this up slightly to make a shallow curve (here, the point was set to Input: 105, Output: 106). When you have completed this step, you should notice a yellow cast in the highlights (Image 4).

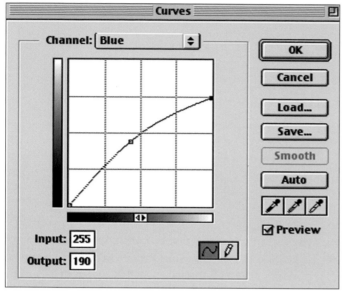

Image 3

Image 4

4. Under channel (at the top of the box), select green (Image 5). Here, we will also reduce the highlight point, although somewhat less (in this example it was set to Input:255, Output: 219). Again, click in the center of the curve and pull up slightly on the line until you start to see a nice, peachy cast in the midtones (Image 6). In this example, the midtone point was placed at Input: 123, Output: 122.

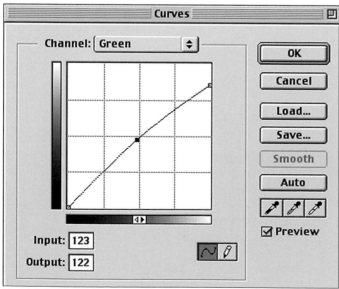

Image 5

Image 6

5. Under channels (at the top of the box), select red. Here, we will leave the highlight point untouched, but add two adjustment points in the midtones, as shown in Image 7. With these points, create a curve that is steep in the highlights but levels out in the shadows. In this case, the top point was set at Input: 191, Output: 159, and the bottom point was set at Input: 70, Output: 46. This operation will add a bluish color cast in the shadows (Image 8).

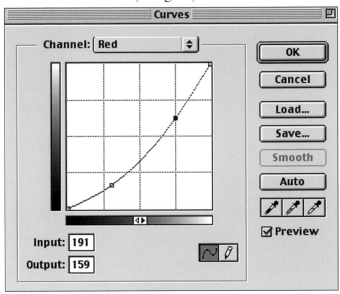

Image 7

Image 8

6. Finally, go to the composite channel (the RGB channel) in the channels pull-down menu at the top of the box. Here, you can adjust the contrast and lightness. You will probably want to boost both of these using a curve similar to the one shown in Image 9. Here, three points were added in the mid/quartertones. The top was set at Input: 182, Output, 209; the middle one was set at Input: 121, Output: 139, and the bottom point was set at Input: 64, Output: 48. For the final results, see Image 10 (next page).

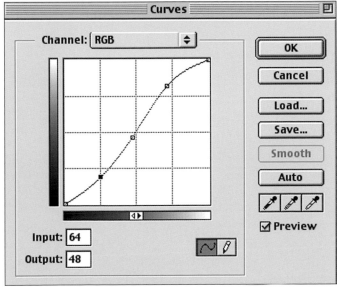

Image 9

6. If you like, you can now flatten and save your image. It's always a good idea, however, to save an unflattened version of your image in case you want to make changes in the future.

Image 10

▶ Variations

There's no reason why this should be the only effect you try with color shifts and the look of cross-processing. Photoshop puts quick tools at your fingertips for creating images you could only dream of producing in the darkroom. Try using the channel mixer to create some wild effects, or employ the hue/saturation controls for interesting color shifts.

If you like, you can now flatten and save your image.

TECHNIQUE 18
BASIC RETOUCHING

▶ **Overview**

Retouching photos is a skill that, especially with traditional materials, requires a great deal of practice to master. Bad retouching looks fake and is easy to spot. While Photoshop doesn't make the job effortless, it makes it much easier. It also permits more experimentation, since errors can be easily eliminated without having to start from scratch.

The topic of photo retouching is a vast one to which entire books have been dedicated. If you plan to do a lot of it, refer to the "additional resources" list for some references to additional resources on this subject. In the meantime, the techniques below will help you address some very common problems.

▶ **Techniques**

Spotting

When photos are printed from negatives, it's not unusual for a speck of dust to fall on the negative or printing paper and cause a small imperfection. Those of us working with scanners experience the same problems with specks and spots, but can remove them easily.

1. Begin with an image in any mode (RGB, CMYK, grayscale, etc.) (Image 1). Look at this image on your screen at a fairly big enlargement (around 200% works well). This is important because, at smaller sizes, the monitor can mask small flaws in the scan. Scroll across the entire image from top to bottom and side to side and look for spots and specks that need to be removed to improve the image.

2. You will undoubtedly find some large and small spots, maybe even a few small fibers that—despite your best efforts to clean the scanner glass and the image surface, still managed to work their way into the scan. The enlarged section of the photo shown in Image 2 is an exaggerated example, since every effort was made

Errors can be easily eliminated without having to start from scratch.

Image 1

to get it dirty before scanning. This would be a lot of work to correct with traditional methods. With Photoshop, it will take just a few minutes.

3. While still zoomed in on the image, select the clone stamp tool on the tool palette.

4. Next, select a brush that is slightly larger than the spot you want to remove. Generally, this should be a very soft brush set to (0%) hardness (to double-check that the brush is set properly, click on the selected brush in the options menu). You may want to use a harder brush if you are correcting an area with sharp details that cannot be softened. In this case, you will need to use the smallest brush possible and be attentive to preserving these details.

5. With your brush selected, go to the spot you want to remove. Locate an area near it (often adjacent to it) with the same color and texture. To take a sample of this area, hold down the Alt/Option key and click on the area with your pointer. Then, move directly over the spot to be removed, release the Alt/Option key and click with your pointer to cover the spot with the material you just sampled.

Image 2

By repeating this technique, you can wipe out most of the spots you come across in an average image. Keep in mind, you can always use the Edit>Undo function or the history palette to step back if you notice a problem as you are working.

This same technique can also be employed to remove small blemishes, bruises or other skin imperfections in portrait photography. You may also find it works well for removing a stray hair.

Quick Tip

You'll notice that this spotting method does not use the "dust & scratches" filter supplied with Photoshop. This is because using that filter results in an often visible loss of sharpness, especially when applied to an entire image.

Softening Lines and Shadows
To soften lines and shadows, follow the instructions given on pages 77–80 for creating a soft focus effect. Since, in this case, you do not want the whole photo to be soft, select a small brush and paint the softness into only those areas where it is needed.

Dodging and Burning
If you've ever gotten frustrated with the trial and error or dodging of burning a print in the darkroom, rest assured that you'll

enjoy the experience in Photoshop much more. With instant previews and undos, the perfect print is much easier to achieve.

1. Select an image in any color mode (Image 1). Keep in mind that, as in the darkroom, neither dodging nor burning can add detail that isn't in the original image (i.e., if a shadow is solid black, you can make it a lighter gray, but can't recapture the texture, etc. that wasn't in the image to begin with). Dodging and burning are most useful for making small changes, such as opening up a shaded area that's just a little too dark, or making an area that is too light just a little less bright and distracting.

2. Decide which regions need to be dodged or burned. In this case, the goat's side where the sun hit strongly could use a little work.

3. Decide what needs to be done. Here, the detail that is present is getting lost, so the goat's shape and texture isn't as apparent as it could be. Sine we are working in a highlight area, we'll need to use the burning tool to darken it slightly.

4. Select the burning tool from the tools palette, and turn to the options menu. In it, there is a pull-down window from which you can choose to burn the highlights, the midtones, or the shadows. It might seem like highlights would be the choice here, but that's not the case. We want the lightest tones to stay light in this area. Instead, the midtones or shadow setting should be used. This will make the details (those areas darker than the highlights) slightly darker, and add a greater appearance of shape and texture (Images 4–6).

Image 3

Image 4
(burn highlights, 20%)

Image 5
(burn midtones, 20%)

Image 6
(burn shadows, 20%)

5. The other selection you need to make in the options menu is the exposure. 10% is probably a good place to start for a small effect. 20% will create an immediately noticeable effect. Over 30% will create a dramatic effect. As you use the tool, experience will become your guide. You can always set the percentage low and make multiple passes (or undo it if you set the value too high).

6. When dodging and burning color images, you need to be very careful to avoid color shifts that may arise due to these manipulations. For example, in Image 6, the hair on the lower front part of the goat's body has taken on a bluish cast due to the burning operation. Fortunately, this problem can usually be corrected easily, provided that the color shift is small (another reason to avoid making dramatic changes with the dodging and burning tool—you may create significant, obvious color shifts). In this case, the selective color control (Image>Adjust>Selective Color) was used to correct the problem (Image 7). Since the problem was in a white area, the color pull-down menu was set to white. The cyan slider was then pulled to the left to reduce the cyan in the whites.

The selective color correction worked well for this particular image, since there weren't a lot of other white areas that could be adversely affected. You could also select the problematic area and use an adjustment layer to correct the color cast.

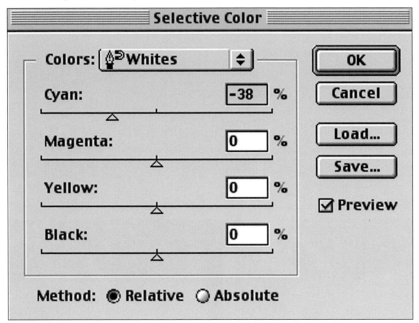

Image 7

Image 8

7. Burning works in the same way as dodging—decide on the problem area, determine which areas need to be lightened (the darkest, middle or lightest tones in the area), and set the dodge tool accordingly. In Image 8, the barn boards in the upper left of the image were dodged. The dodge tool was set for highlight, in order to leave the shadows untouched and bring out the wood texture revealed in the lighter areas.

Cloning to Conceal Problems

Here's a problem that would be hard to correct with traditional methods. This photo (Image 9) was taken from a fast-moving train in Portugal, and a railway marker ended up in the lower left corner. It could be removed by cropping, but the composition seemed better if the width of the image could be retained.

Image 9

Fortunately, a few corrections in Photoshop can usually solve this type of problem.

1. Begin with an image in any mode (grayscale, RGB, CMYK, etc.).

2. Look closely at the problematic area and determine if there are other areas in the photograph that have some or all of the same elements in the same light. In this case, a tree trunk, part of a road and a piece of shrub need to be replaced. Fortunately, all of these elements are repeated in the same light in the adjacent parts of the image. This makes it a good candidate for this technique. If there are no good replacements within the image, you may need to get creative. If you took more than one image of the scene (or have other images of similar scenes), you may be able to use elements from these.

3. Once you have decided on the raw material you will use to conceal the problem area, select it. Then copy and paste it to a new layer in this image. You may have lots of layers when you are done. Here, three new layers were needed (Image 10). The first

> This makes it a good candidate for this technique.

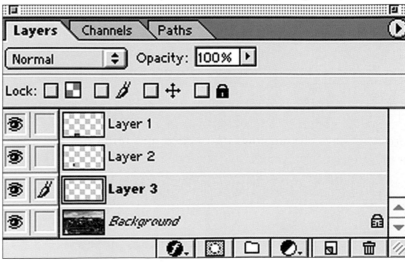

Image 10

contains a sample to be used to "rebuild" the road, the second contains material for the tree trunk and grass, and the last contains part of a shrub.

4. Zoom in on the problem area and move the material on the closed layers roughly into position over the area to be concealed by them. (Image 11). As you can see, things will probably look pretty rough at this point.

5. If you have more than one layer or element to work on, decide on the one that should be tackled first, and click off the visibility of the other layers (click on the eyeball next to each one in the layers palette to do this).

6. Beginning with this layer, you'll need to determine what changes need to be made to make it match up as seamlessly as possible with the photo around it. The following are some common problems and their possible solutions:

Image 11

Problem:	Solution:
Lines don't match up	Use the distort function (Edit>Transform>Distort) to better align the layers. The rotate tool may also help (Edit>Transform>Rotate).
Colors don't match	Use the curves (Image> Adjust>Curves) on the new layer to coordinate the colors.
Obvious lines at edges of selected area	Use a soft brush with the eraser tool to remove the edges of the selection, or with the clone stamp tool to create a softer transition between the new and original material.
Contrast doesn't match	Use the curves (Image> Adjust>Curves) to coordinate the contrast of the new layer with the original.
Lighting direction doesn't match	If the lighting is reversed left to right, reverse the layer left to right (Edit>Transform>Flip Horizontal). Check to make sure this doesn't cause other problems (like reversed text). If the lighting is otherwise mismatched, try utilizing the lighting effects filter (Filter> Render>Lighting Effects).

For this image, the first step was to get the road in place. With only the road layer and background visible, the distort (Edit>Transform>Distort) and rotate (Edit>Transform>Rotate) tools were used to line up to edges of the road in the new layer with the edges of the road in the background image. Then, the clone stamp tool was set to 50% opacity (in the options menu) and used to blend the edges of the new selection into the background. A small amount of burning was also needed to make the tones match up properly.

The next step was the tree trunk. After making this layer visible, the parts of the new tree trunk layer that overlapped the completed road retouching were simply erased. The layer was set to 90% opacity, to reduce its brightness and allow it to blend in better with the background.

Finally, the shrub layer was made visible. As with the tree trunk, the extraneous material in the layer was first erased. Then, the clone stamp tool was used to blend the new layer with the existing background.

Using these techniques and careful attention to detail, you can create surprisingly good results in just a few minutes (Image 12).

Image 12

TECHNIQUE 19
CATCHLIGHTS

• •

▶ Overview

Catchlights, those glistening bright highlights, make eyes look vibrant and alive. Without them, portraits often look dull and unattractive. If you didn't get a good catchlight in your original image, it's easy to add it in Photoshop. This technique can also be easily adapted to add nice highlights to just about anything. To maintain a sense of realism, keep the surface characteristics in mind when creating the catchlight. Under the same light, an apple (smooth surface) and a peach (dull surface) will have very different highlights. If you're not clear on this, refer to the lighting books in the resources list in the appendix.

▶ Technique

1. Begin with an image in any mode (Image 1).

2. Using the magnifying glass tool, zoom in very close on one of the subject's eyes.

3. Create a new layer (Layer>New>Layer) on which to paint your catchlight.

4. Set white as your foreground color (unless you want the catchlight to be another color).

5. Select the airbrush tool and an extremely small, soft brush (here a three-pixel brush with 0% hardness was used). With it, draw the rough shape of the catchlight on the new layer over the subject's eye. Again, this will be much easier if you are zoomed in tightly on the eye. The drawing does not have to be perfect.

6. Select the smudge tool. Depending on your light source, select a brush. If your lighting is hard, select a harder brush to keep better defined edges on the catchlight; if your lighting is soft (like the cloudy sky here), you can use a softer brush. In the menu, set

Image 1

. . . this will be much easier if you are zoomed in tightly on the eye.

Use the smudge tool to push and pull your catchlight . . .

the pressure of the smudge tool to about 50%. Use the smudge tool to push and pull your catchlight into just the shape you want (Image 2). The correct shape and position for the catchlight will depend on your light source and its relationship to the subject. Here, since a cloudy sky was the source, a relatively large, soft catchlight was created in the upper left portion of the eye.

6. When you are happy with the catchlight, duplicate the layer and drag the second layer over the other eye. (This is the best way to ensure that the catchlights are identical in each eye.)

7. If you like, you can reduce the opacity of the new layers to reduce the appearance of the catchlight. In Image 3, the layers were set to 90% opacity.

Image 2

Image 3

TECHNIQUE 20
MOTION BLUR

▶ Overview

When longer shutter speeds are employed, cameras have the ability to capture images of motion as the human eye could never see it. If you missed it in the original image (or never had it, but want to create the illusion of motion), Photoshop makes it easy.

▶ Technique

1. Begin with an image in any mode (Image 1).

2. Identify the areas in the image where you want to apply the motion blur, and decide in what direction the blurs should go (Image 2).

3. Use the lasso tool to select one of the areas. Accuracy is not very important here. The blur will obscure a lot, and what it doesn't cover can be quickly removed later.

Image 1

Image 2

4. Copy the selected area and paste it into a new layer. Repeat steps three and four for each of the areas to which you want to add a motion blur (here, three).

5. When you've made all your selections, activate one of the new layers by clicking on it in the layers palette.

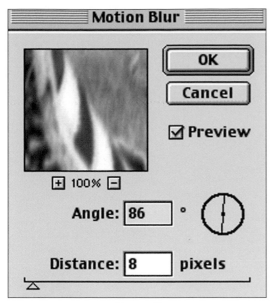

Image 3

6. Go to Filter>Blur>Motion Blur. Using the direction guide and slide in the motion blur palette you can control direction and extent of the blur (Image 3). Think carefully about each before applying the motion blur. Clicking on the preview box to activate it will be very helpful.

7. Repeat step 6 for each of the layers you created in steps 3 and 4. When you have completed adding the motion blur effect to each of the layers, you may want to make the background invisible (click off the eyeball next to it in the layers palette) (Image 4). Then, use the magnifying glass to zoom in on the blurred layers and make sure they don't contain anything that shouldn't be blurred (anything that was actually stationary in the image). If you find anything, just use the eraser tool to eliminate it.

8. Turn the background visibility back on. If you like, adjust the opacity of any of the layers to reduce the blur effect (Image 5).

Image 4

Image 5

TECHNIQUE 21
COMPOSITING

▶ Overview

If you've ever tried to combine two images in the darkroom, you know that creating a seamless effect is extremely tricky. In fact, one of the earliest popular uses of digital imaging was to create composite images more easily and with more immediate control.

The basic techniques and controls used for digital compositing are presented below. The precise needs of your image (and your intent) will dictate, to a large degree, which methods you employ and in what manner you use them.

▶ Techniques

1. Begin with two or more images in any mode (Images 1–2). The criteria for selecting these images should be very rigorous. For realistic compositing, the direction and quality of lighting should be very similar in all of the elements to be combined. While you can make some adjustments, it also helps if the elements to be combined are properly exposed and contain no major color problems. Additionally, check to make sure the focus is correct. If you put a softly focused subject in the midst of a sharply focused group, any hope of creating a realistic effect in the final image will be lost.

Image 1

2. Look at the images carefully and decide which one contains more of the material you want to retain in the final image. In this case, the theater (Image 1) will be the background. The only part of the other image (Image 2) that will be used is the figure in the center of the frame.

3. Carefully select the material that will be imported into the background photograph (Image 3). This may be trickier than it sounds. Use whatever combination you need of the marquee, lasso and magic wand tools, and don't forget that you can add to and subtract from selections. If you don't feel you are fully up to speed on making selections in Photoshop, this would

Image 2

Image 3

be a good time to consult a basic Photoshop manual and run through a tutorial.

4. When you have completely selected the area that will be moved to the background image, you will generally want to feather this selection (Select>Feather). This will soften the edges of the selection and make them a little less obvious when you move the selected area into the other image (Image 4). Feathering the selection about two pixels is usually a good place to start, although you may decide that one or three works better for you. If you want some cheap insurance, you can also save the selection at this point (Select>Save Selection).

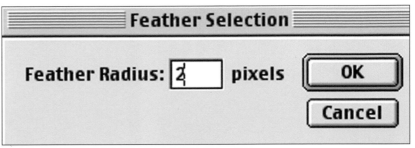

Image 4

5. Copy the selected area (Edit>Copy) and paste it (Edit>Paste) into a new layer in your background image (Image 5).

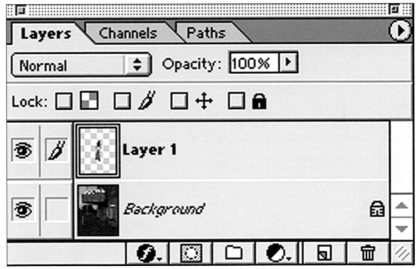

Image 5

6. Once this is done, the rest of the job of compositing is fine tuning the components to make them blend as seamlessly as possible. A good place to start is with the correct positioning of the new element on the new layer. To do this accurately, you'll need to consider a few things. First, look at the scale of the imported material. Does it need to be changed in order to make sense with the subjects around it? If you think the scale is pretty good, think about perspective. If your background image (as here) shows a scene in the distance, the subject must be at a correct size in relation to its apparent distance from the camera. In Images 6 and 7, you can see the difference between reasonably good perspective

(Image 6) and obviously wrong perspective (Image 7). In each image, the figure size remained the same. Only the position was changed.

Image 6

Image 7

7. Next, look at the color, brightness and contrast of the new element in relation to the background. Here, the contrast on the woman is a little high, and she's a bit bright. Both of these problems were corrected using the curves (although you could also use one of the other image adjustment controls to do the same thing). Image 8 shows the that was curve applied, and Image 9 shows the result.

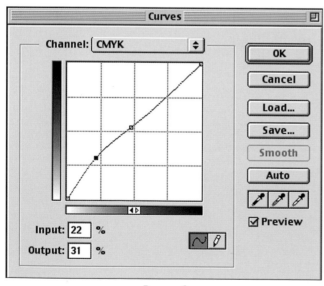

Image 8

Image 9

8. As a result of feathering the selection (which worked well almost everywhere), there are a few spots with a little extra material around the edges (Image 10). After zooming in on these

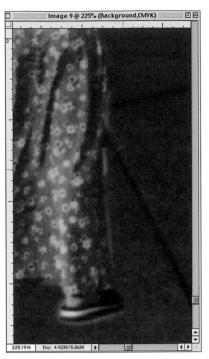

Image 9 @ 225% (Background,CMYK)

Image 10

areas, the extraneous material can simply be nicked off using the eraser tool.

9. With the image almost complete, all that's missing here is a shadow (this may not be needed for every image). Everything else in the image has long, relatively dark shadows, and adding one to the imported subject will help the realism of the effect.

To add a drop shadow, duplicate the new layer in the layers palette. Click on the duplicated layer to activate it. To make the figure of the woman black, go to brightness/contrast (Image> Adjust>Brightness/Contrast) and set both of the sliders to -100. Next, go to Edit>Transform>Distort and drag the top of the new layer down to the side (Image 11). In this case, since the shadow needs to bend up a wall, a selection also needed to be made of the area of the shadow that would be on the wall. The distort function was used a second time to adjust this area.

With the basic outline of the shadow in place, a small Gaussian blur (Filter>Blur>Gaussian Blur) set to five pixels helped to create a softer edge on the shadow (Image 12).

Image 11

Image 12

COMPOSITING 119

10. The final step is to make the shadow more transparent by reducing the opacity of the layer it is on. In this case, the opacity was set to 30% (Image 13).

Image 13

The final step is to make the shadow more transparent . . .

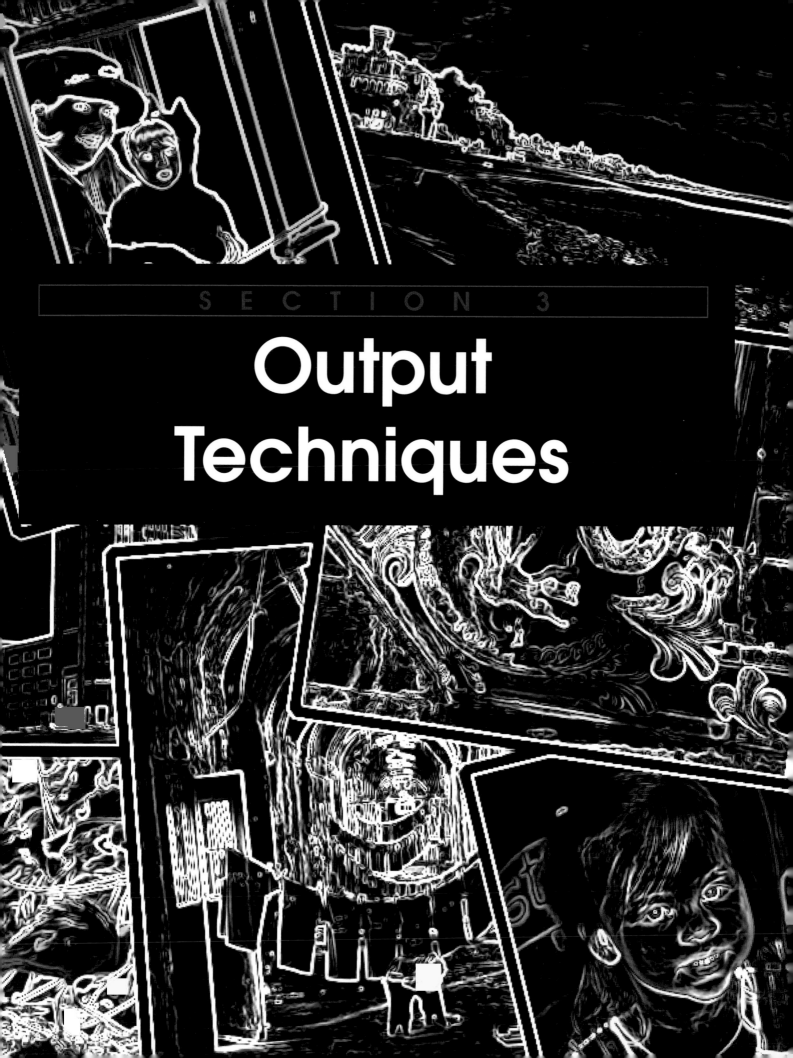

Output
Techniques

Output Techniques

Outputting your images is the last step in digital imaging. For some people, this may mean uploading the images to a website or e-mailing them to friends, to others it may mean creating a print or a negative from the digital file. For most people it is probably a little of both.

▶ Internet or E-mail

When using your images on the Internet (either in web pages or as e-mail attachments for on-screen viewing), two factors must be kept in mind: quality and file size.

If your image will only be viewed on screen, you should set the resolution at 72 dpi (standard screen resolution). Anything higher will create a larger file without increasing the appearance of the image. To create even smaller images (ones that will load more quickly on web pages), consider compressing the image by saving it in the TIF or JPEG format. In the TIF format, you can use LZW compression (termed a "lossless" compression because it does not destroy data in the image). The JPEG format, in contrast, uses what is called a "lossy" compression (meaning data *is* lost, but perhaps not objectionably so). Using images in the RGB mode (or grayscale mode for black & white images) will also provide smaller file sizes than using them in the CMYK mode.

Before deciding, experiment with the options and decide where you personally are most willing to compromise—file size or image quality.

▶ Desktop Printing

The quality and accessibility of photo quality printers for home use has improved dramatically over the past few years. While Epson is the leader in this field, Canon, Hewlett Packard and Apple offer excellent models as well.

For true photo quality output, look for a printer that can render your images at 1440 dpi, and which offers software that provides you with good control over the output. Reading through

The JPEG format, in contrast, uses what is called a "lossy" compression . . .

the manual for your printer will provide you with the details you need to create an image of the appropriate resolution and size for optimum print quality.

For best results, consider a printer that uses more than four inks (models that use six are widely available). You should also invest in appropriate paper for high-resolution printing.

▶ Output to Film

A film recorder is a device that creates a negative from your digital file. This is normally a service you would seek from a color lab. Outputting a color negative requires very large, high resolution files, so check with your service provider before preparing your files. The size of the print you want to create from the negative will also be a factor in deciding what size negative (and therefore what size digital file) is required.

▶ Other Professional Printing Services

There are literally dozens of methods for creating prints from your digital file, and many of these (due to the cost of the equipment) are best accessed through an imaging lab or professional printer. For single prints or other small quantity jobs, an imaging lab is your best bet. For high volume jobs (over 500 pieces), seek out the services of a professional printer. In either case, if it is at all possible, decide on the method of output *before* you prepare your file. Consult your service provider for guidelines of file preparation and advice for the best output device for the results you hope to achieve.

▶ Digital Back to Traditional

If (despite the fun you have with Photoshop) you still like to get back into the darkroom once in a while, consider outputting your own paper negatives. Simply invert your finished image (Image>Adjust>Invert) to create a negative you can output on your desktop printer. In the darkroom, place the negative ink-side up on your printing paper for a softer, more textured look, or ink-side down for a sharper look. (For printing ink-side down, you may want to reverse your digital file left to right by going to Edit>Transform>Flip Horizontal before printing. This will preserve the correct orientation when you print through it.)

> Outputting a color negative requires very large, high resolution files . . .

Quick Tip

The longevity problems associated with digital prints have for a long time steered people away from using them. Archival materials promising longevity comparable to traditional color prints are now available, but only time will tell if they live up to their promise. To be safe, note that inkjet prints are very sensitive to water—one drop and they are ruined. Handle them carefully. As with traditional photos, you can expect the best longevity from your digital prints when they are displayed out of direct sunlight.

Additional Resources

► General Photoshop Instruction

Adobe Creative Team. *Adobe Photoshop 6 Classroom in a Book* (Peachpit Press, 2001).

Blatner, David and Bruce Fraser. *Real World Photoshop 6* (Peachpit Press, 2001).

Haynes, Barry. *Photoshop 6 Artistry* (New Riders Publishing, 2001).

McLelland, Deke. *Photoshop 6 Bible* (Hungry Minds, 2001).

Rose, Carla. *Sam's Teach Yourself Adobe Photoshop 6 in 24 Hours* (Sam's, 2000).

Schrand, Richard. *Photoshop 6 Visual Jumpstart* (Sybex, Inc., 2000).

Stanley, Robert. *Complete Idiot's Guide to Adobe Photoshop 6* (Que, 2000).

Willmore, Ben and Becky Morgan. *Adobe Photoshop 6.0 Studio techniques* (Adobe Press, 2001).

► Color Management

Margulis, Dan. *Professional Photoshop 6: The Classic Guide to Color Correction* (John Wiley & Sons, 2001).

► Digital Photo Retouching

Lute, Gwen. *Photo Retouching with Adobe Photoshop* (Amherst Media, 2000).

► Scanning Techniques

Sheppard, Rob. *Basic Scanning Guide for Photographers and Other Creative Types* (Amherst Media, 2001).

Williams, Robin and Sandee Cohen. *Non-Designer's Scan and Print Book* (Peachpit Press, 1999).

► Digital Photography

Sheppard, Rob. *Computer Photography Handbook* (Amherst Media, 1998).

Eggers, Ron. *Basic Digital Photography* (Amherst Media, 1998).

► Black & White Imaging with Photoshop

Schaub, George. *The Digital Darkroom: Black & White Techniques Using Photoshop* (Silver Pixel Press, 1999).

► Lighting Techniques

Kerr, Norman. *Lighting Techniques for Photographers* (Amherst Media, 1998).

Montizambert, Dave. *Creaitve Lighting Techniques for Studio Photographers* (Amherst Media, 2000).

► Traditional Photographic Techniques

Roger Fremier. *Techniques for Black & White Photography: Creativity and Design* (Amherst Media, 2000).

Wildi, Ernst. *Composition Techniques from a Master Photographer* (Amherst Media, 2000).

Index

Wedding Photography

Creative Techniques for Lighting and Posing, 2nd Ed.

Rick Ferro reveals the techniques behind his signature style. New edition in full color with updated text and images. $29.95 list, 8½x11, 128p, 75 color photos, index, Ferro. (ISBN 1-58428-046-8) Order no. 1649

FEATURES:
- Techniques for dramatic lighting
- Over fifty lighting diagrams
- Organizing every step of the shoot
- Studio and environmental portraits
- Posing for individuals, couples and groups

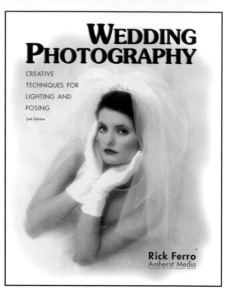

Outdoor and Location Portrait Photography

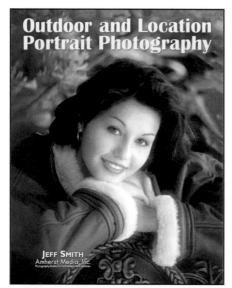

Outdoor portraiture offers a professional photographer countless opportunities. Learn to select the best equipment, identify the perfect light, pose your subjects and create beautiful portraits. $29.95 list, 8½x11, 128p, over 60 color and b&w photos, index, Smith. (ISBN 0-936262-80-X) Order no. 1632

INCLUDES:
- Responding to lighting situations
- Finding ideal light
- Finding the perfect scene
- Composing the foreground, background and subject
- Urban, architectural and nightscape portraits
- Marketing outdoor portraits

Corrective Lighting and Posing Techniques for Portrait Photographers

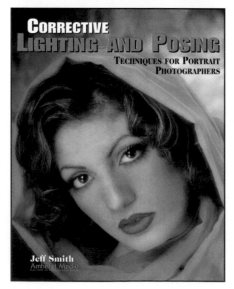

Bring out the best in your clients through effective lighting and posing strategies for flattering portraits. $29.95 list, 8½x11, 128p, 100 full color photos, index, Smith. (ISBN 1-58428-034-4) Order no. 1711

FEATURES:
- Evaluating your client's problem areas
- How to address your concerns with tact and professionalism
- Utilizing corrective lighting to optimize subject's appearance
- How to adapt poses to hide flaws, like a double chin or tummy bulge

Other Books from
Amherst Media

Computer Photography Handbook

Rob Sheppard

Learn to make the most of your photographs using computer technology! From creating images with digital cameras, to scanning prints and negatives, to manipulating images, you'll learn all the basics of digital imaging. $29.95 list, 8½x11, 128p, 150+ photos, index, order no. 1560.

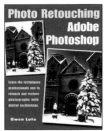

Photo Retouching with Adobe® Photoshop®

Gwen Lute

Designed for photographers, this manual teaches every phase of the process, from scanning to final output. Learn to restore damaged photos, correct imperfections, create realistic composite images and correct for dazzling color. $29.95 list, 8½x11, 120p, 60+ photos, order no. 1660.

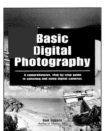

Basic Digital Photography

Ron Eggers

Step-by-step text and clear explanations teach you how to select and use all types of digital cameras. Learn all the basics with no-nonsense, easy to follow text designed to bring even true novices up to speed quickly and easily. $17.95 list, 8½x11, 80p, 40 b&w photos, order no. 1701.

Basic Scanning Guide For Photographers and Creative Types

Rob Sheppard

This how-to manual is an easy-to-read, hands on workbook that offers practical knowledge of scanning. It also includes excellent sections on the mechanics of scanning and scanner selection. $17.95 list, 8½x11, 96p, 80 photos, order no. 1708.

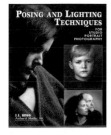

Posing and Lighting Techniques for Studio Photographers

J.J. Allen

Master the skills you need to create beautiful lighting for portraits of any subject. Posing techniques for flattering, classic images help turn every portrait into a work of art. $29.95 list, 8½x11, 120p, 125 full color photos, order no. 1697.

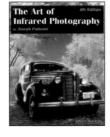

The Art of Infrared Photography, 4th Edition

Joe Paduano

A practical guide to the art of infrared photography. Tells what to expect and how to control results. Includes: anticipating effects, color infrared, digital infrared, using filters, focusing, developing, printing, handcoloring, toning, and more! $29.95 list, 8½x11, 112p, 70 photos, order no. 1052

McBroom's Camera Bluebook, 6th Edition

Mike McBroom

Comprehensive and fully illustrated, with price information on: 35mm, digital, APS, underwater, medium & large format cameras, exposure meters, strobes and accessories. A must for any camera buyer, dealer, or collector! $29.95 list, 8½x11, 336p, 275+ photos, order no. 1553.

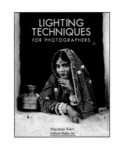

Lighting Techniques for Photographers

Norman Kerr

This book teaches you to predict the effects of light in the final image. It covers the interplay of light qualities, as well as color compensation and manipulation of light and shadow. $29.95 list, 8½x11, 120p, 150+ color and b&w photos, index, order no. 1564.

Creative Lighting Techniques for Studio Photographers

Dave Montizambert

Gain complete creative control over your images. Whether you are shooting portraits, cars, table-top or any other subject, you'll learn the skills you need to confidently create with light. $29.95 list, 8½x11, 120p, 80+ photos, order no. 1666.

Composition Techniques from a Master Photographer

Ernst Wildi

In photography, composition can make the difference between dull and dazzling. Master photographer Ernst Wildi teaches you his techniques for evaluating subjects and composing powerful images in this beautiful full color book. $29.95 list, 8½x11, 128p, 100+ full color photos order no. 1685.

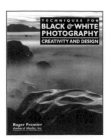

Techniques for Black & White Photography: Creativity and Design

Roger Fremier

Harness your creativity and improve your photographic design with these techniques and exercises. From shooting to editing your results, it's a complete course for photographers who want to be more creative. $19.95 list, 8½x11, 112p, 30 photos, order no. 1699.

Handcoloring Photographs Step-by-Step

Sandra Laird & Carey Chambers

Learn to handcolor photographs step-by-step with the new standard in handcoloring reference books. Covers a variety of coloring media and techniques with plenty of colorful photographic examples. $29.95 list, 8½x11, 112p, 100+ color and b&w photos, order no. 1543.

Special Effects Photography Handbook

Elinor Stecker-Orel

Create magic on film with special effects! Little or no additional equipment required, use things you probably have around the house. Step-by-step instructions guide you through each effect. $29.95 list, 8½x11, 112p, 80+ color and b&w photos, index, glossary, order no. 1614.

Portrait Photographer's Handbook

Bill Hurter

A step-by-step guide to portraiture that leads the reader through all phases of photography. This book will be an asset to experienced photographers and beginners alike. $29.95 list, 8½x11, 128p, full color, 60 photos, order no. 1708.

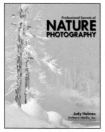

Professional Secrets of Nature Photography

Judy Holmes

Covers every aspect of making top-quality images, from selecting the right equipment, to choosing the best subjects, to shooting techniques for professional results every time. $29.95 list, 8½x11, 120p, 100 color photos, order no. 1682.

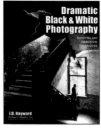

Dramatic Black & White Photography:
Shooting and Darkroom Techniques

J.D. Hayward

Create dramatic fine-art images and portraits with the master b&w techniques in this book. From outstanding lighting techniques to top-notch, creative darkroom work, this book takes b&w to the next level! $29.95 list, 8½x11, 128p, order no. 1687.

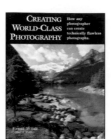

Creating World-Class Photography

Ernst Wildi

Learn how any photographer can create technically flawless photos. Features techniques for eliminating technical flaws in all types of photos—from portraits to landscapes. Includes the Zone System, digital imaging, and much more. $29.95 list, 8½x11, 128p, 120 color photos, index, order no. 1718.

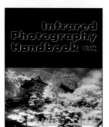

Infrared Photography Handbook

Laurie White

Covers black and white infrared photography: focus, lenses, film loading, film speed rating, batch testing, paper stocks, and filters. Black & white photos illustrate how IR film reacts. $29.95 list, 8½x11, 104p, 50 b&w photos, charts & diagrams, order no. 1419.

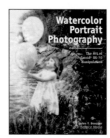

Watercolor Portrait Photography: The Art of Manipulating Polaroid SX-70 Images

Helen T. Boursier

Create one-of-a-kind images with this surprisingly easy artistic technique. $29.95 list, 8½x11, 120p, 200+ color photos, order no. 1698.

More Photo Books Are Available

Contact us for a FREE catalog:
AMHERST MEDIA
PO BOX 586
AMHERST, NY 14226 USA

www.AmherstMedia.com

Ordering & Sales Information:

INDIVIDUALS: If possible, purchase books from an Amherst Media retailer. Write to us for the dealer nearest you. To order direct, send a check or money order with a note listing the books you want and your shipping address. Freight charges for first book are $4.00 (delivery to US), $7.00 (delivery to Canada/Mexico) and $9.00 (all others). Add $1.00 for each additional book. Visa and Master Card accepted. New York state residents add 8% sales tax.

DEALERS, DISTRIBUTORS & COLLEGES: Write, call or fax to place orders. For price information, contact Amherst Media or an Amherst Media sales representative. Net 30 days.

1(800)622-3278 or (716)874-4450
FAX: (716)874-4508

All prices, publication dates, and specifications are subject to change without notice.

Prices are in U.S. dollars. Payment in U.S. funds only.